Praise for *Just Open the Jar*

"Raw-truth light bulb moments! Remember that you can make dreams come true when you bet on you!"

—Robin Wilson, Founder, Clean Home Design

"For those of us without the luxury of a clean slate, *Just Open the Jar* is a breath of fresh air. Paula Blankenship shows us how to create something beautiful and deeply authentic—without blowing up our lives to do it. If you're ready for a fresh start, this is your paint and paintbrush to design the life you actually want to live."

—Lauren Wittenberg Weiner, Founder, WWC Global,
and National Bestselling Author, *Unruly*

"When big changes take your life by storm, this is the must-have read to restart your life."

—Chuck Garcia, Leadership Coach; Professor, Columbia
University; and Author, *The Moment That Defines Your Life*

JUST OPEN THE JAR

JUST OPEN THE JAR

A DIY Path to Creating a Life You Love

PAULA BLANKENSHIP

Matt Holt Books
An Imprint of BenBella Books, Inc.
Dallas, TX

The events, locations, and conversations in this book, while true, are re-created from the author's memory. However, the essence of the story, and the feelings and emotions evoked, are intended to be accurate representations. In certain instances, names, persons, organizations, and places have been changed to protect an individual's privacy.

Matt Holt is an imprint of BenBella Books, Inc.
BenBella Books, Inc.
8080 N. Central Expressway
Suite 1700
Dallas, TX 75206
benbellabooks.com
Send feedback to feedback@benbellabooks.com

Matt Holt and *BenBella* are federally registered trademarks.

Printed in the United States of America
10 9 8 7 6 5 4 3 2 1

Library of Congress Control Number: 2025053310
ISBN 9781637749081 (hardcover)
ISBN 9781637749098 (electronic)

Editing by Lydia Choi
Copyediting by Evan Herrington
Proofreading by Lisa Story and Sarah Vostok
Text design and composition by PerfecType
Cover design by Morgan Carr
Cover image © Adobe Stock / salita2010 (both)
Printed by Versa Press

Dedicated to my loving mother, Clarice Blankenship.

Your unwavering love, endless support, and unshakable belief in me, even when I didn't deserve it, gave me the courage to become who I am. Forever your greatest fan, always.

CONTENTS

INTRODUCTION

In 2011, I was a forty-eight-year-old single mom praying my thirteen-year-old son wouldn't get thrown out of the expensive private school I was busting my ass to afford, and wondering if, after a lifetime of entrepreneurism, I'd ever find stability.

Today, I'm the owner of Heirloom Traditions Paint, a company that generates $33 million in annual sales and stands as one of a handful of women-owned businesses in the paint and coatings industry. Forbes has called me the "Queen of Paint." I've won a 2024 EY Entrepreneur of the Year East Central Award and received the Gold Stevie Award for Manufacturing.

Not bad for a high school dropout who started mixing paint in her kitchen.

You see, paint isn't just a product to me. It's possibility. It's also always been my destiny. From my earliest days painting in the back of my mom's furniture store to decorating million-dollar interiors, I've always seen the world through an artist's eyes. But it wasn't until I started mixing paint in my kitchen, trying to give my son something productive to do, that everything clicked into place. My mom taught me that everyone has something valuable to share, and I've built my company on that belief. I've created not just a product but a community where people support each other's creative journeys. My paint comes in sample jars as a way to encourage others to try out something new. When someone opens one of our jars for the first time, they're not just opening paint. They're opening a door to transformation.

A long time ago, I learned it was important not to get hung up on the possibility of messing up. I saw how an accidental splotch of paint could be the beginning of a new and more interesting design than what I'd set out to put on my canvas. Eventually, I applied that lesson to my journey as an entrepreneur, and to my personal life as well. When I dove headlong into a new business venture that later went bust, I chose to see it not as a failure but as a chance to learn through trial and error. Just like when I wound up in a situation many people around me called a mistake—like getting pregnant out of wedlock—I quickly realized it was actually the greatest gift I'd ever received.

Embracing creativity, and believing in my ability to make something that contains value, is the foundation of the philosophy that has guided me throughout my life, in art, business, and some of my most private moments: *Just open the jar.*

"Just open the jar" means being unafraid to unlock transformation. It means being willing to try something new. And it means doing it at any time in your life—even after fifty, like me.

• • •

Years ago, I was not your stereotypical picture of success. I grew up in Oneida, a small town in rural Tennessee with more churches than opportunity. I dropped out of high school and never got a college degree. My parents wanted me to take over their furniture store business, but I turned my nose up at it. I thought furniture was boring. I had bigger ambitions. Or so I thought.

As you'll see, my professional journey has had plenty of detours, dead ends, and unexpected discoveries. I opened a clothing store for teens with my sister when I was still a teen myself. I designed leather stage wear for country music entertainers in Nashville and got to go on tour with one of the industry's most famous stars. I started a manufacturing business, scored a million-dollar order, and then just as quickly had to shut it all down. Those are just a few examples.

I flirted with big money and glamour only to learn that I wanted to work with real people—with family, or people who felt like it. I moved away from my hometown only to realize that I missed it, then moved away for good when I realized I had to save myself and my son. The place we landed is where Heirloom Traditions Paint was born.

I went full circle, from swearing off furniture to making paint that embellishes it.

My all-in-one paint has everything in one, so that my customers don't have to rely on people at a hardware store to purchase the right prep. I limit the color options to the best ones, so it's easier for people to make better decisions. I also use my social media channels to educate people on paint, color, prep, and process.

Our paint works on leather, fabrics, cabinets, exterior surfaces, interior surfaces—you name it. And the best part? There is no primer, sealer, or sanding required. It has this incredible bonding power that allows it to adhere to almost any surface. It's also flexible, so it won't crack or break apart over time. It can handle heat and sun exposure, making it perfect for front doors and outdoor projects.

That's been its claim to fame, and it truly delivers on that promise.

But Heirloom Traditions Paint is not just a major business. It's also a lifestyle. I have 1.5 million Facebook followers, five hundred thousand of whom are in the private Heirloom Traditions Paint Facebook group, where I engage, interact, and teach painting techniques on a weekly basis. There, people post before-and-after photos of their DIY projects and get advice and encouragement from fellow members. The results aren't always something that could be showcased in *Better Homes and Gardens*, but they're real, and that's the point.

Transformation doesn't have to cost millions. It can start with a single jar.

Our customers are retirees rediscovering purpose, worn-out executives wanting to get their hands dirty, or families teaching their kids not to throw something out just because the color faded. They invite their friends, they post their projects, and they keep us growing. We now ship hundreds of thousands of orders every year.

I believe people already have everything they need inside them to change their lives. They just need the right tools, a little direction, and the courage to start. Because here's the bigger truth behind what those little jars represent: You don't have to gut your life and rebuild it from the ground up to create something beautiful. Sometimes, you just need to paint over it.

A lot of people think transformation means demolition. That to change your home—or your business or your life—you have to tear it all down, burn bridges, walk away from everything you've known, and start over. But that's not how it works for most of us. Especially not the women I serve.

Most of us are juggling kids, jobs, relationships, aging parents, bills. We don't have the luxury of a clean slate. But we *do* have a room full of old furniture, or a kitchen we're tired of looking at, or a life that feels a little worn around the edges. That's where paint comes in. It's a fresh start *without* a full do-over.

You don't have to rip out your cabinets. You don't need to replace your furniture. You just need to open the jar, pick up a brush, and begin.

That's how most of our customers start. One small project. One tired dresser or chipped chair they'd been thinking of tossing. And once they see the transformation, they start looking around for what else they can renew. They grow more confident. They stop second-guessing themselves. They stop asking for permission. And soon, they're not just painting furniture—they're painting a new picture of who they are.

We show people that transformation is possible—without a contractor, a big budget, or a degree in design. You don't need to be an expert. You don't need to wait for the timing to be perfect. You just need to start.

That's what I did with my own life. I've been able to embark on so many different business ventures, start so many new chapters, because I wasn't afraid of just opening those jars. Some beginnings were harder than others, especially in my personal life. But ultimately, through practice, and by cultivating confidence, I was able to continually change and adapt. Sometimes, I had to start from scratch. More often, I had to work with what I already had. And over time, with every stroke, every setback, every lesson—I built something beautiful.

That's what I want for you too. You don't need to change everything to change your life. You just need to open the jar.

• • •

In the following pages, I'll take you through the wild, colorful, and often unpredictable journey that led me from a tricycle in my parents' furniture store to building a multimillion-dollar paint brand. My story is about taking creative leaps without letting fear of failure stop me. At its heart, this book is about trusting your instincts, making beauty out of messes, and believing—deeply—that you can shape your life with your own two hands.

In "What Does Opening the Jar Mean?" you'll see how, from watching my mom transform discarded furniture into something beautiful, to learning embroidery from a neighbor and entering craft contests, I grew up with the confidence to trust my hands and ideas. That early support—and my mom's example as a savvy, fearless businesswoman—gave me the courage to take my first big leap: opening a clothing store at sixteen. It wasn't perfect, but it was my first real "open the jar" moment.

Next, in "Why You Just Need to Get Started," I share how a chance encounter with country music star John Schneider gave me the courage to take a leap I wasn't sure I was ready for—and how that leap set everything in motion. I'd never made a leather outfit before, but when John asked me to design one for him, I said yes anyway. That "just get started" moment led me to win a national leather competition and, eventually, to dress another huge country music star, and this time for the cover of *Spin* magazine—all because I dared to dive in before I felt fully prepared. But I also learned the flip side, that starting something doesn't mean you're locked in. Sometimes you have to know when to walk away.

In "Sometimes the Simplest Idea Is the Best," I talk about coming home to Oneida after a few years on the road designing leather outfits for country stars, thinking I was giving up on adventure. Instead, I stumbled into something even more lasting. It's about how my sister and I finally gave in to the thing we'd resisted our whole lives: the family business. What started with a van full of carpet rolls turned into something much bigger, and taught me that sometimes the most obvious, unglamorous ideas are the ones that actually work.

In "Back to the Drawing Board," I walk you through the wild turn my life took after my divorce—when I had no job, no plan, and no choice but to start over. What began as a scrappy little side hustle selling painted candleholders turned into a full-blown manufacturing business—and then a million-dollar order. But just when I thought I had it all figured out—business partners lined up, a move to Cleveland in the works, everything falling into place—life threw me the biggest curveball yet.

"Coloring Outside the Lines" is about the time I came home at thirty-two, pregnant, unmarried, and completely lost. I thought my life was over, that all the momentum I'd built was gone. But that little boy in my arms, my Brady, would turn out to be the reason I would rebuild everything better than before.

In "When Paint Peels Back," I take you back to the day a flashy New Yorker with slicked-back hair and a tank top walked into the little store in Oneida I was running and asked me to furnish a house—*by tomorrow*. That wild, whirlwind project was the start of a six-year roller coaster with a millionaire who taught me more about business than any MBA ever could. One minute I was decorating log cabins in Tennessee, the next I was designing for *Fortune* 500 companies in Connecticut. But while my career was soaring, my personal life was crumbling. Success on the outside hid a darker private reality, and getting out of that took every ounce of strength I had.

In "Starting Heirloom," I tell the story of how a simple act—painting an old dining table—turned into the start of the defining business of my life, though I had no way of knowing that at the time. I was in a new city, trying to give my son a better future and find my way after some tough years. Painting helped me feel like myself again, and when I shared my projects on Facebook, the response shocked me. That interest led me to an old family paint plant in Louisville, and soon I had my first product, my first color card, and my first customer.

In "Scaling Up," I walk you through the moment this little side hustle of mine turned into something much bigger. What started as a fun after-school project with Brady suddenly became our family's best shot at stability when Craig—my new boyfriend and eventual husband—very abruptly lost his corporate job. With no choice but to make it work, we doubled down. Orders were growing, but so were the challenges. I realized we needed a better product and a new strategy.

In "Ditching the Middleman," I tell the story of how we finally made the leap to direct-to-consumer. After years of chasing retail deals with companies like hardware and other lifestyle retailers, we realized those stores weren't actually putting our products on the shelves—and in some cases, they were breaking contracts and selling our paint online at a discount. That was the tipping point. I tore up a big order and said, "We're doing this ourselves." We learned how to run Facebook ads and shot live videos to connect directly with our community.

In "Staying the Course," I share how a burst of creativity nearly pulled me off track—and how learning to focus saved everything. Right after our first big breakthrough with Facebook ads, I invented a travel pillow that took off like wildfire, landing me on TV and almost in global airport stores. But chasing that success nearly derailed the paint business I'd worked so hard to build. With Craig's steady voice in my ear, I made the hard choice to walk away from the pillow and double down on what was already working.

Finally, in "Full Circle," I tell the story of how I eventually bought out the factory that manufactured paint for me—and, in a twist of fate, sold part of it back to the man who first helped me get started. This chapter is about taking back control, learning to steer your own ship, and doing business with integrity even when it's hard. It's also about loyalty—not the kind that keeps you stuck, but the kind that lets you look back, reach out a hand, and lift someone else up. Because sometimes, the most powerful thing you can do is return the favor.

Every life is different. I don't presume to have all the answers. All I can do is share what I've done and what's worked for me, and hope that some of it inspires or resonates with you. I promise you honesty. Many business books will try to offer you the world. I know that's not possible. My offer is more modest but potent. Small, incremental changes through things that you control.

I'm a woman in business who's navigated marriage, divorce, and motherhood, and all the ways those major life experiences can collide with your work, sometimes creating obstacles, sometimes giving it all meaning.

I created Heirloom Traditions Paint to help my son adjust to a new school, a new city, a new life. I wanted to help him take control of his world. I didn't realize that, along the way, it would also change my life.

So if you take one thing from this book, let it be this: You don't have to know everything before you begin. You don't have to have the whole path mapped out. You don't need a million-dollar loan or a shiny degree or someone else's permission. You just need to take the lid off.

That's what *Just Open the Jar* means. It means starting where you are, with what you have. It means believing that even something as small as a brush and a can of paint can lead to something much bigger. Whether you're revamping an old dresser or rebuilding your life from scratch, the magic doesn't happen until you make the first move. You don't need a guarantee. You just need a little faith—and the courage to start.

So trust yourself. And open the jar.

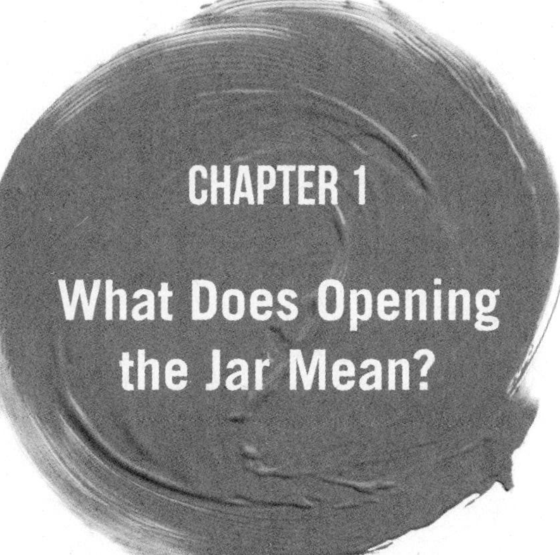

CHAPTER 1

What Does Opening the Jar Mean?

The first person I saw wield a paintbrush was my mom. Clarice Blankenship would place rub-on decals of beautiful little lambs or bears on the heads of secondhand cribs and baby beds, and delicately paint them with the care of Michelangelo in the Sistine Chapel. She handed the beds out for free to her furniture store customers when they were expecting a child.

My mom was only 5 feet, 2 inches tall but commanded a room with her presence. She had a 100-watt smile that drew people in like moths to the light. People loved her. She was sweet, and she really listened. Customers walked into the store and lingered, confiding in and unburdening themselves to my mom for far longer than the time of a transaction. She let them pay on credit when they were going through tough financial times. Business, she knew, was all about relationship building, and she understood the value of kindness and empathy.

That didn't make her a pushover: She was an astute businesswoman who could spot an opportunity from a mile away. Back in the 1950s, she opened the first drive-through restaurant in town, serving food out of paper containers for people on the go—which might not sound like anything grandiose today, but it was an absolute novelty at the time. Later, when she met my dad, they teamed up to try something new.

Gilbert Blankenship was a 6-foot-5 heartthrob who did infrastructure work building bridges for the State of Tennessee. Before meeting my mom, he'd mostly driven and operated a pile driver used for building bridges. He was a quiet man who dreamed of striking it rich by drilling for oil. He didn't have a shred of business experience but had plenty of moxie. One day, he went out and bought a secondhand sofa for next to nothing, and brought it home. My mom took one look at it and saw its promise. She stayed up all night reupholstering it with fresh, new fabric, transforming a banal piece of furniture into a real treasure. The next day, my parents sold it for $100. Then my dad went hunting for another couch. They quickly realized they could sell greater quantities by buying used furniture from nice hotels, which frequently remodeled to keep looking new and modern. My dad would drive 500 miles to Chicago, load up his truck with sofas, armchairs, and tables, then speed back to my mom, who would decide which pieces could be sold as they were and which ones she should refurbish. Within a few months, they'd moved their operation into a brick-and-mortar building on Main Street. And that was the beginning of the furniture business my parents would run for the next forty years. Its success would become the linchpin of all the businesses they eventually owned. It's also the start of my story.

As a kid, my parents' furniture store was my world. My earliest memories are of me whizzing down the aisles on my tricycle while my mom chatted away with her customers. Because my sister, Sherry, and I spent so much time with our mom in there, she made sure it was a comfortable space for us. She set up a craft room in a little apartment she had built behind the store, and set us loose painting, drawing, airbrushing T-shirts, and making stained glass pieces.

I took after my mom. I loved painting and decorating as much as she did. I watched her closely as she transformed drab furniture into real works of art, then set out to do the same with my crafts. "Paula is my artist daughter," she'd say when she introduced me to customers and acquaintances, beaming with pride. She always praised my work. It was one of her earliest gifts, and one that shaped the future of my life and career. She taught me to believe in myself, to have faith in my hands and their ability to create beauty.

She also encouraged me to learn from others. Our neighbor who lived on the opposite side of the road was a woman whose husband was sick with tuberculosis. I visited often to keep her company, and when she realized I had a knack for crafts, she taught me how to embroider, quilt, and use her old treadle sewing machine. I'd go over almost every night after dinner to make doll clothes and furniture and yarn flowers. My parents would leave our porch light on so that I could make my way back as late as I chose, sometimes close to midnight. Encouraged by my mom and my neighbor, I entered craft-making contests and started racking up awards.

All of this is to say that from a very young age, I was blessed to have mentors who inspired and motivated me to be creative, to experiment, and to trust my burgeoning sense of aesthetics and style. I learned to be bold and to not get hung up on the possibility of messing up. I grew to not even think of messing up as failure. A blot of paint or a splotch of glue in the wrong place could be repurposed to design something even more interesting than what I'd set out to do, and if not, I could just try again. This faith in my imagination and what my hands could do with it became the foundation of the philosophy that would go on to guide the rest of my life, in art, business, and some of my most private moments.

"Just open the jar" means deciding to take a leap without knowing exactly where you'll land. Art and business both demand a kind of courageous creativity. Success in either realm starts with an innate trust in yourself, a drive to try something new without being paralyzed by the fear of failure. If you're fortunate, you've had people along the way who nurtured that daring spirit, who believed in your potential even before you fully did. Not everyone is lucky in that way, and sometimes that belief has to be self-generated, drawn from some quiet place within. Simply opening the jar—beginning without overthinking, without fearing mistakes—is itself an act of bravery that you can cultivate through repetition. It's the first step toward keeping your creativity alive, instead of letting the pressure to be perfect, or the fear of being out of your depth, shut it down.

• • •

My mom made it her mission to make Sherry and me believe that we could do whatever we set our minds to. "There is no job, no business, no dream too big for you," she would tell us time and time again. That might not sound like much, but let me tell you: For someone growing up in Oneida, Tennessee, it was everything.

Oneida is a speck of a town wedged in the Cumberland Plateau, founded in the late nineteenth century by a group of railroad executives from New York. It started out as a simple train depot but was catapulted into a boomtown when loggers and miners flooded the area in the early 1900s. That was when my great-grandparents arrived and set up a hotel. In the late 1920s, when US Highway 27 was built and sliced through town, fewer and fewer trains came in, and Oneida started to fizzle out. The miners and loggers moved on. Only a fraction of blue-collar workers remained—stuck there, you could say. My grandparents opened the first restaurant on Main Street in the 1940s and called it Crystal Cafe. Every item on their menu was homemade and raised or grown on their farm. Like them, the people who stayed in Oneida got by with hard work and grit, but it wasn't always easy. Today, Scott County is one of the poorest counties in the United States.

Fewer than four thousand people live in Oneida, but you'll find a church on nearly every block. Oneida is smack-dab in the Bible Belt. People look out for each other, but they also keep score. Your choices, style, or ambitions can get you talked about fast. There are few opportunities, and you basically have two options: Stay in line or leave. If you're a girl with big ideas, who doesn't want to marry young, or who dares to dress differently or dream louder than what's usually acceptable, you might ruffle some feathers.

And I happened to be an unusual bird.

I don't know if I was born different or if my mom's education made me that way. In addition to encouraging me to be creative, from the time I was six, she took Sherry and me on exotic vacations far away from the Cumberland Plateau, and I'm not talking California. We went to Tahiti. Venezuela. Portugal. Spain. She wanted us to know the world was vast and full of surprises. She didn't want us to be small-minded. That was another gift she gave me: I could see beyond the borders of my world. But that meant not always fitting in. And nowhere was that clearer than at school.

I hated school. I was bored out of my gourd. Today, I could say that was due in large part to being dyslexic and probably having a touch of undiagnosed ADHD. I hated busywork and being told what to do, and reading and writing were a torment. Letters and numbers danced across the page. I did well in science because we got to draw—the human body, cells, plants, that kind of thing—and that, I excelled at. I was a visual learner at a time when little to no consideration was given to different kinds of learning.

Just about the only thing I enjoyed about school was deciding what to wear every morning. As a teen, my love of art had expanded into a love of fashion. I loved trying on funky clothes and colorful shoes—loafers in different textures, leathers, suedes, and bold colors. The other kids at school all wore tennis shoes. I wasn't consciously setting out to be different, but I rolled in like a peacock. One year for picture day, I wore a dark green velvet blazer with a Madras plaid tie—like a man's necktie but styled for women. I also convinced the photographer to get my cousin in the shot, and lord knows why he agreed.

"You're a big fish in a little pond, girly," my brother, Michael, would tell me. Michael, my mom's son from a previous marriage before my dad, was more than a decade older than me and extraordinarily brilliant: He'd graduated from high school two years early, at sixteen, and gone on to become the top graduate at the University of Tennessee before getting recruited by a huge accounting firm in Miami.

"All right, so what would you do if you were me?" I'd ask him defiantly.

"Well, if I were you, I would do my best to get into any Ivy League school and leave," he'd say.

That made sense for Michael, who had a scholastic brain. But not for me. I was barely scraping by in school.

For a while, I got away with it. My mom was so consumed with her own hustle—running stores, flipping houses—that she trusted me to take care of myself. She'd bought me a car when I was just thirteen so I wouldn't have to spend three hours a day on the bus after we moved out of town, and gave me a charge account so I could feed and clothe myself, which made me even more independent than I already was. I didn't want to bother her with my grades, so I forged every report card signature from the sixth grade on. I'd tell her, "I made all A's," and she'd say, "Great, honey."

By the time I was a senior, I realized I didn't have enough credits to graduate, and I was told I'd need to attend summer school to get my diploma. *To hell with it*, I told myself. *I'll just take the GED and move on.* I was more than done with school by then, and besides, I had my sights set higher.

Through my mom's example, I'd long seen how you could marry creativity and business. I remembered watching her draw up a financial statement for the bank; she had over a million dollars in assets, which back then, and to me, was a number so big I could hardly fathom it. I decided to follow in her footsteps. So at just sixteen years old, I opened my own clothing store.

• • •

I called the store Bargain's Bazaar, and it was a secondhand clothing shop I ran out of one of my mom's buildings. It was equal parts thrilling and chaotic; often it felt like playing dress-up in a dollhouse. I opened and closed the store whenever I pleased, had little idea how to balance a ledger, and missed so much school my teachers soon caught on. Turns out it's tough to fake sick when half the town can watch you strut into your own store at ten in the morning.

Bargain's Bazaar gave me a taste of what it was like to work in sales, but it also made me realize I needed help. I needed people who complemented my skill set.

Sherry had always shared my love of clothes. On weekends, we'd hop in the car and drive around hunting for discount stores and thrift shops, always on the lookout for hidden gems—jackets, especially. One afternoon, we wandered into the S&S Bargain Store. It was the kind of place you could easily overlook, but something about the racks of affordable, stylish clothes caught my attention. I'm the kind of person who'll strike up a conversation with anyone, so I marched over to the owner and asked how he kept his prices so low.

He told me the secret: All the clothes were returns from Spiegel, a catalog company that didn't bother restocking returned merchandise. Instead, they sold it in bulk to other retailers for pennies on the dollar—anything to avoid the cost of repackaging. I turned to Sherry. "We could do this," I told her. "We could buy Spiegel returns and sell them ourselves."

We rushed home and pitched the idea to our mom, who immediately offered to clear out one of her buildings and set up racks. Our dad was more resistant. "Oh gosh, girls, don't get into clothes, the rags business," he said. If you buy twelve pieces wholesale and sell six at full price, he explained, you've just broken even. Then the remaining six go on sale, and you never actually make a profit. Plus, with theft, tied-up money, and unsold inventory, it was simply a terrible business, he said. "Sell furniture," he encouraged. "They never go out of style."

"No," we insisted. "That's boring. That's all y'all have ever done."

We were young and convinced we could do it differently. So despite his warnings, our dad handed us $10,000 in cash to get started. I closed Bargain's Bazaar and together with Sherry opened Tags Unlimited, the first clothing store selling exclusively teen fashion in Oneida.

Our roles were clear from the start. I was the idea person—the one out front buying, selling, decorating, and dreaming big. Sherry was the backbone—quiet, steady, crunching numbers. She kept the books, paid the bills, made sure we didn't collapse under our own enthusiasm. We made a good team because we respected what the other brought to the table. I put on the show. She made sure the lights stayed on.

Ultimately, our dad wasn't wrong about the clothing business—it was hard to turn a profit, and we didn't. But it served as a crash course in entrepreneurship and a blueprint for how Sherry and I work together. It was where we learned to run a business, solve problems, and trust our instincts. Plus, we got to keep all the cutest clothes.

Opening clothing stores was my first real "open the jar" moment. It was the first time I combined my interest in business with my love of art and creativity. If I'd waited until I had a business degree, a perfect business plan, or even a high school diploma, I'd still be twiddling my thumbs. Instead, I opened my first clothing store at sixteen. I didn't know what I was doing, not really, but I wasn't afraid to try my hand at something new, and I trusted my innate sense of style. I was right, too: Soon I was spending more time with my classmates' moms than my classmates themselves, because I was selling them clothes their kids, my peers, now wore.

So what does opening the jar mean? It means taking the first messy, imperfect, possibly irrational step toward something that's been sitting on your heart. We all have these jars in our lives—ideas, dreams, changes we keep thinking about, talking about, planning for. Don't put them off indefinitely. As you'll see in the following pages, taking chances on my own occasionally harebrained ideas has led me down roads I never expected to travel. Some of those experiences were tough. Others were rich and fulfilling. But they all taught me lessons that would prove invaluable when I built the business that now defines my life.

1. **Don't overthink it: Just open the jar.** Success begins with taking that first step without being paralyzed by fear. I didn't wait until I had a business degree or even a high school diploma before opening my first store at sixteen. Lord knows I had no idea what I was doing, but I trusted my eye for fashion. My mom taught me that failure isn't something to fear—it's just part of the creative process. So don't get stuck in your head waiting for the perfect moment. Just open that jar and see what happens.
2. **Find people who complement your strengths.** I learned early on that I couldn't do everything myself. When Sherry and I opened Tags Unlimited, we divided responsibilities naturally. I was the peacock out front—buying, selling, decorating, and dreaming up what could be. Sherry was the backbone—quiet, steady, making sure the numbers added up and the bills got paid. We succeeded because we respected what the other brought to the table. I put on the show, and she kept the lights on. Don't try to

be everything to everybody. Find your strengths, and surround yourself with people who fill in the gaps.

3. **Let curiosity take you beyond your borders.** My mom didn't just encourage me to create. She showed me the world was bigger than Oneida. In a town where most people stayed in line or left, I became an unusual bird. I wore velvet blazers and Madras ties when everyone else wore hand-me-down tennis shoes. And ultimately, my nonconformist streak is what would help me develop an eye for fashion and decorating, and launch me on my entrepreneurial path. Being willing to look beyond your borders—whether that's your hometown, your industry, or your comfort zone—is what keeps your creativity alive. Don't let fear of standing out keep you from spreading your wings.

CHAPTER 2

Why You Just Need to Get Started

Sherry and I were running Tags Unlimited when my aunt invited us to a multilevel marketing conference, the kind where they put on a big show about financial freedom and opportunity. I wasn't particularly interested in that kind of business, but I'd heard the demo was impressive, and to be completely honest, I'd also heard that "Handsome Ken" would be there—Ken Mackovic, the owner of Olde Worlde Products out of Greensboro, North Carolina. I went, and sure enough, Ken lived up to the hype. He was charismatic, confident, the kind of guy who could sell you anything. We started dating not long after that.

Ken had a light yellow Rolls-Royce he drove around. One day he invited me to tag along to an event in Owensboro, Kentucky, at a place called the Executive Inn down by the water. When we got there, we realized John Schneider—Bo Duke of *The Dukes of Hazzard* himself—was performing in the ballroom at the same time as Ken's event. Ken asked me which I'd rather attend. I wasn't a big country music fan—I was more of a dance music kind of girl; Motown and Whitney Houston were more my speed—but I made a few choice exceptions, and John Schneider was one of them. Ken got me a ticket.

That evening, I arrived late to the show. Everyone was already seated around lovely tables set with white linen cloths in a sort of dinner theater setup. I handed my ticket to the maître d', who smiled at me more enthusiastically than I would have expected and escorted me all the way across the room down to a table front and center, by far the best seat in the house. Everyone watched me go. I figured it was one of the only seats left. John put on a great show, and when it was over, I left.

The next morning, down at breakfast, I was walking past a long, busy table when I heard someone call my attention. "Hey, hey, hey," a deep voice said. I turned, tray in hand, and found myself face-to-face with John Schneider himself. "You were seated at my table last night," he said.

"I was?" I asked.

"You were mistaken for my girlfriend."

Well, that explained the fancy treatment. We laughed and chatted a few more seconds before saying goodbye and parting ways.

A few hours later, Ken was pulling up in his yellow Rolls-Royce to take us home when lo and behold, who comes striding up to the car? John again. He admired Ken's wheels and then saw me. "It's you!" he called. "It's me," I acknowledged, and once more we parted ways—for the last time, surely, I figured.

Flash forward a few years. In addition to Tags, Sherry and I had embarked on a few other small business ventures, including airbrushing T-shirts, which is what we were doing at a little country music venue in Parkers Lake, Kentucky, when who do I see stroll onstage? You guessed it. John swung around a pole and started singing his latest hit. Right in the middle of the song, he saw me, stopped singing, and shouted, "Well, hey! How are you?"

After the show, someone came to get me, saying John wanted to talk. I climbed into his tour bus parked by the stage.

"So what do you do? You airbrush T-shirts?" he asked.

"Actually, I work with leather," I answered.

Not long before, I'd been browsing a catalogue and spotted a beautiful leather belt I'd considered ordering until I saw how much it cost: The price was exorbitant. So I thought, *I'll just make it myself.* I got in touch with a shoemaker in Oneida I'd known all my life, a kind and older man, and asked him to show me how to work leather. He taught me, and then I made my belt. From there I'd started experimenting with wallets and bags as well.

"You should make me something," John said.

"What do you want?" I replied.

He thought about it for a moment. “A leather outfit. Out of chamois leather. No fringe on the right sleeve, because it’ll get in the way of my guitar strings,” he said.

I said I’d do it. And then realized what I’d done.

I’d never made a leather outfit in my life, never mind for a celebrity. I was absolutely out of my depth. But I looked around the bus’s small enclosure, found a stray napkin, sketched a design, and then measured John.

A few months later I drove to Nashville along with two girlfriends for moral support and to show off my skills: I’d dressed one of them in another leather outfit I’d made. I handed John his outfit, and he pulled it on. It fit him like a glove.

I’d pulled off my gambit. I was thrilled. As I basked in the glow of my success, John and I kept chatting, and that’s when he informed me that he was giving up his singing career to get married and move out to California. *Hell*, I thought, *there goes my walking billboard*.

But mixed with the disappointment was a realization. I’d made John Schneider a beautiful outfit that fit him perfectly, even though I’d never made a garment before. And let me tell you, putting a zipper on a pair of leather suede pants is not easy. That victory gave me the fuel to do something I thought I’d never do.

I decided to go back to school.

If opening a clothing store at sixteen was my first "just open the jar" moment, this was what I call my "just get started" moment. I instinctively realized that if I admitted I'd never made a leather outfit before, or if I suggested I needed to do a trial run, John might have lost interest. I would have never had the chance to actually learn on the job and prove to myself that I could do it. Of course, this wasn't a complete leap into the unknown: I had acquired a baseline set of skills to work with leather, and that's what gave me the confidence to try something more ambitious. Designing for someone like John Schneider was an opportunity I simply couldn't pass up, even if I didn't feel 100 percent prepared.

It was time to dunk my paintbrush into the jar I'd opened. I just had to get going.

It paid off. Even though John never became the walking billboard I'd hoped he might be, my experience with him opened the door to the next phase of my leather venture, as you'll see. Plus, as I found out much later, that first outfit didn't go to waste. John and I stayed in touch over the years, and not long ago in 2023, I ended up remodeling his house in Nashville. I asked him about the outfit then. He told me it was hanging in the music museum beside Graceland in Memphis, Tennessee.

• • •

I enrolled in a design school in Franklin, just outside Nashville. But I didn't go to learn about fashion. I already had years of experience experimenting with style at my clothing stores, Bargain's Bazaar and Tags, and I was actively teaching myself how to work with leather. Besides, I didn't believe anyone could teach me about taste. You have it or you don't. I didn't need to pay an institution several grand to tell me which colors or shapes went best with each other.

That was why I signed up for interior design, the other option at the school. Interior design, something I had less experience with, seemed like the more practical choice. And it made my mom, who still hoped that one day I'd get into furniture like her, happy.

The real reason I went to design school in Franklin was more strategic. I figured that if I could get closer to Nashville, the world capital of country music, I might have a shot at dressing other stars. And even though I didn't really believe in them, I knew most people thought degrees conferred credibility. So I played along, going to my interior design classes—but what I was really invested in was what I did after school, in the privacy of the dingy apartment I shared with a few other girls off campus, where I experimented with leather late into the night.

I started bringing some of my pieces to class to show my professors. Soon enough, I caught the attention of a woman named Patricia who'd been a costume designer at Opryland

USA and taught in the fashion design department. She pulled me aside one day and said I had something. She told me about this scholarship the Leather Institute of America was offering—some national competition for students doing standout work with leather. You had to draw a design, and if the institute liked it, they would give you the money to buy the leather and make the actual outfit. And you'd get to keep it. Just as my childhood neighbor and my elementary school teachers had encouraged me to put my talents to the test and compete in local craft fairs years ago, Patricia suggested I throw my hat in now as a young designer.

I sketched a design for a teal leather skirt and top, submitted it, and ended up winning. I wasn't even in a fashion program! It was another jolt of validation, and I started getting even more creative with my designs.

I'd been playing with the idea of using leather as a canvas for avant-garde art. I'd airbrushed T-shirts, which could result in beautiful and original designs, but you could only get so much money for that. A cotton shirt simply was not worth a lot. Other kinds of garments could get you more buck for your bang. You could sell a denim jacket, for instance, for a few hundred. And leather for even more. If I placed my designs on the back of a leather jacket, I could charge a few thousand. The medium was more precious, and the process more labor intensive. On top of being more fashionable, working with leather made more business sense. So I came up with my own system out of appliqué. I bought a Singer embroidery machine to sew these pieces of leather down very neatly onto the jacket so they looked seamless. The designs rested so flat on the jackets they looked like paintings.

For the first jacket I made, I found a paper napkin in a shop, maybe a Hallmark gift store, by an artist who specialized in cubist designs, featuring an angular woman and man dancing on a black-and-white floor; very art deco. I decided to re-create that image in leather on the back of a pale-pink lambskin jacket. I drew the whole design out on very thin pieces of leather, cut them up like puzzle pieces, and sewed them on the jacket's back using my appliqué process. I then placed a small string of real pearls around the woman's neck.

For another jacket, I decided to re-create a picture I found in a magazine showing champagne exploding out of the top of a bottle by a woman's red lips. I don't think I picked up on the sexual connotation at the time, but my objective was to catch a man's attention, and it worked. I used red piping and red leather lacing around it. I now had two showy jackets, as flashy as the outfits I used to parade down the hall in high school. I decided I was ready to start showing them off. But not to my professors at design school. This time, I wanted to go straight to country music stars.

But first, I had to find them. There was no Google back then. I sat hunched over the phone book and inspected each page, looking for publicists or anyone associated with singers in the Nashville area. I had my eye on one in particular.

As I've mentioned, deep down I wasn't a huge country fan. I just knew country singers were my target audience because I liked to dress like them. But there was one artist whose music melted my heart. Tanya Tucker had this wild energy, a mix of toughness and vulnerability that was magnetic. As a teenager, I owned exactly one country album, and it was Tanya's. I listened to her duet with Glen Campbell, "Shoulder to Shoulder," about a thousand times when I was seventeen. I remember thinking, *If I could design for anyone, it'd be her.* Not necessarily because she was the biggest star, but because something about her, both her style and the way she looked unflinchingly at the camera on her album covers, spoke to me.

I'd been trying to track her down for months, dropping by record labels uninvited, hoping someone would let me show them my jackets and point me in Tanya's direction. I left messages and handed out cards, to no avail. One day I met a stylist who'd dressed a lot of artists, including Tanya, and she handed me her number. Heart pounding, I called. No one answered. Another dead end.

I went back home to Oneida for spring break, feeling somewhat dispirited about my leather venture but also more generally about school. Looking back, design school was filled with a lot of people who loved the idea of being a designer more than they loved the work itself. There were maybe two or three students who really stood out, who had that spark, that drive, but the rest struck me as a bunch of kids whose parents had money and were just buying them a degree.

Along with that, I realized that completing my interior design course wasn't enough to graduate. I had to enroll at a separate college to cobble English and math credits as well, which I had absolutely no desire to do. My initial motivation was melting away. I felt the same as I had in high school, that school simply wasn't for me.

I was wondering what to do when one day, the phone rang.

"Hey, this is Tanya Tucker. I'm doing a shoot for the cover of *Country Fever* magazine tomorrow, and I need an outfit. Can you help me?"

The words formed themselves before I even had time to think. "Come on over," I told her.

I'd been hoping for this moment for so long, but not unlike the time I agreed to make John Schneider a leather outfit even though I had no experience, I was suddenly seized by panic. This time, it wasn't because I wasn't up to the task. My problem was much more mundane. It was a Sunday afternoon in rural Tennessee in 1997. Nothing was open. No fabric stores, no boutiques. And I needed fabric, fast.

Then I had an idea. I jumped in my car and raced to Walmart—pretty much the only place still open—and bought every car towel I could get my hands on. They were made of chamois, the same soft material I'd used to make John Schneider's suit. I could do it again for Tanya Tucker.

I got home right as Tanya was pulling into my driveway in a black Mercedes with tinted windows and a license plate that read "MS.BADASS." Tanya stepped out of her car like a queen, then unloaded a bunch of clothes from her trunk, as well as—I'm not joking—a ring-necked pheasant she'd just shot on someone's farm. It still had a little blood on it.

We said hello to each other, and she instantly put me at ease. She told me she'd just checked out of a rehab clinic. I was stunned. Her song "Love Me Like You Used To" was topping the charts. "They're calling it my comeback song," she said with a shrug, then added, "I don't know where the hell I've been." We both laughed.

Once inside my house, I dug through the clothes she'd brought and found a leopard print two-piece bathing suit. Then I took a beautiful chamois dress she'd tossed in and, without hesitation, cut it in half. Tanya didn't bat an eye. I turned the top half into a cropped jacket using the material from Walmart and fringed out the bottom into a thong-style skirt to be worn over the bathing suit.

Tanya looked fierce in her photo shoot.

After that, I didn't go back to design school. I started touring with Tanya instead.

It was a wild time. I met everybody and anybody on the road, and I got to design for other country stars too. It was the best exposure I could hope for: My jackets were literally onstage.

But I quickly realized that life on the road simply was not the life I wanted. It all felt like a high-end carnival—city after city, same show, same script. We'd sleep all day, perform at night, grab a late meal, then collapse in another faceless hotel room. After a while, you forgot what town you were even in. I didn't drink or pop pills like most of the crew, which made me the odd one out. It was lonely. Behind the glaring lights and the roaring crowds, there was a kind of emptiness.

I started to miss Oneida deeply. I missed real people and real connections. I decided it was time to go back.

There's a misconception in business that says if something *looks* successful, you should hold on to it with both hands—even if it doesn't feel right. I don't buy that. When I was on tour with Tanya, I was technically living the dream, but I was disconnected from myself.

Here's what I learned and what I want to pass on to you: You just need to get started. But you also need to know when to quit. Just because something is working doesn't mean it's right. Designing leather outfits for country music stars was a wonderful opportunity, but I knew it wasn't sustainable for me. It wasn't allowing me to put down roots and grow as either an artist, an entrepreneur, or as a person either. I didn't want to be a side act in someone else's show forever. I wanted to build something of my own—something rooted in real creativity, real craftsmanship, and real connection, and something that reflected my values. Heirloom Traditions Paint would be exactly that, but to get there, I had to learn a few more lessons along the way.

1. **You don't have to be ready—you just have to be willing.** If you wait until you feel totally ready, you'll never do a damn thing. When John Schneider asked me to make him a leather outfit, I had no business saying yes—I'd never made a single garment, let alone for a celebrity. But I said yes anyway. Why? Because something in me knew I'd figure it out. I sketched the design on a napkin and learned as I went. And it turned out beautifully. So here's what I want to tell you: Stop waiting for permission. Don't wait for the perfect moment. Just start. Say yes to the thing that scares you a little.
2. **Starting opens doors—even if they don't lead where you thought.** I thought designing that outfit for John was going to launch my career with him, that it would be my big break. It wasn't. He quit singing and moved to California. But that single act of saying yes, of getting started, led me down a completely different path: to design school, to a national leather competition I won, and eventually to dressing Tanya Tucker. The point is, getting started

doesn't guarantee you'll end up where you think you're going, but it does get you moving. And once you're in motion, doors open. People notice. New ideas come. So don't get stuck waiting for the "right" opportunity. Make a move—any move—and see what happens.

3. **Movement creates momentum.** I didn't wake up one day and decide to become a designer for country stars. It started with one belt. Then a bag. Then a jacket. None of it was mapped out. I just kept experimenting and following my curiosity. Every small step led to the next. You don't need some big, grand plan to get going. You just need to do the next little thing in front of you. Try the idea. Make the call. Send the email. Cut the fabric.

Sometimes the Simplest Idea Is the Best

After two or three years on the road designing leather outfits for country music stars, I filled my car with my sewing machine and remaining pieces and drove back home to Oneida. As I've mentioned, my decision to return was largely guided by a desire to get back to something real and put down some roots. Sherry had just had her first son, and something about that shifted my perspective entirely. I wanted to be around to see that baby grow up, to be part of his life. At that point, I never dreamed I would have a child of my own. I simply thought that wasn't in the cards for me. Most people I'd gone to school with had ended up marrying their college sweethearts. My one attempt at higher education had only lasted a semester, and finding a husband had never been part of the plan. The only available people left in Oneida were divorcés and people like me, who'd just kind of missed the bus.

Not that I was desperate to settle down; a part of me realized that if I'd gone down that path, I would have never had the opportunity to get into design and travel the region the way I had for the last few years, and I relished the independence and adventure it had provided me. I didn't want to give that up. Besides, my immediate sights were set on building a new business.

While the glamour of working with stars like Tanya Tucker was undeniable, it hadn't provided a stable income. Creating custom pieces for performers was feast or famine—a big payday when someone commissioned an outfit, then weeks of hustle trying to land the next gig. I needed to pivot to something more reliable. The girl was growing up and having real money problems.

Sherry and I had closed Tags Unlimited by then. We'd finally acknowledged the fact that our dad had been right all along: There's no money in clothes. It really was the "rags business," as he'd called it. The logic he'd presented us with held true: If you buy twelve pieces of clothing and sell six at full price, you've just broken even. Then the remaining six get marked down, and suddenly you're fighting just to recoup your investment. Plus, seasons change, styles shift, and sizes run out.

"But sofas never go out of style!" he always told us, to which we'd royally rolled our eyes. "Furniture is boring," we'd shoot back. Our parents' business seemed as exciting as watching paint dry on a wall. But at long last, we were maturing and heeding the siren call of the family business. If running clothing stores had felt like child's play, and dressing and touring with music stars was like some sort of rebellious adolescence, then finally coming into the furniture business was like entering adulthood. We decided to give it a shot.

But not just yet: Our mom was still running her own furniture store, and we didn't want to compete with her. She suggested we get into a complementary business. "People who buy furniture generally buy floor coverings too," she said. If Sherry and I opened up a floor covering store, she'd send us her customers.

It just so happened that an older and childless relative had recently passed away and left Sherry and me each $5,000. Instead of blowing it, we decided to use it as seed money.

We drove down to Georgia to buy carpet rolls directly from carpet mills, loaded our dad's van, hauled them back, found someone to lay carpets in people's homes, and opened a store. Before we knew it, we had a real business on our hands.

Floor covering wasn't sexy, but it was stable—that floor covering store is still in operation today, over forty years later. The money came in steadily rather than in unpredictable bursts, like it had in my leather design days. It also allowed me to work closely with Sherry again, who brought the baby to work. We set up a little nursery in the store just like our mom had set up a craft space for us in her furniture store years ago. Sherry's son took his first steps there.

I was shocked by how much motherhood had changed my sister. We used to love shopping, driving hours just to browse new boutiques for fun. Now, suddenly, she didn't care about clothes for herself—only for the baby.

Working with family can obviously have its stresses. It can bring out a certain sense of competition and sharpen existing sibling rivalries. But the bulk of my experience working with my sister was enriching and fulfilling. We complemented each other wonderfully—Sherry with her numbers brain, me with my people skills—and I got to help with the baby.

Our floor covering business did so well, we soon realized we had to expand. When a large, dilapidated building came up for sale on Main Street close to our mom's store, we saw an opportunity. The place was in terrible shape: Birds were literally flying through it, and the back half was flooded. But in the same way my mom had trained her eye to divine a worn-down piece of furniture's potential, I was learning what you could unlock in a seemingly unusable space. Sherry and I bought the building and got to work. We put on a new roof and cleaned the space out.

Then, shortly after we settled in, our mom announced she was retiring. Our grandmother, her own mom, needed full-time care and didn't want outside help, so our mom decided to move in with her. Our dad wasn't the type to step into the business; he'd spent his career in the oil fields and had no interest in the daily grind of retail. So Sherry and I stepped in and finally took up the family furniture legacy.

Sometimes, the simplest ideas—or the most familiar—are the best. For years, we had resisted the very thing we grew up around, thinking we needed to invent something new or chase something flashier to make our mark. But returning to the family business wasn't settling—it was a kind of coming home, not just geographically but also creatively and personally. What once seemed boring and old-fashioned suddenly revealed itself as solid, reliable, and even rich with opportunity. I wasn't giving up on my creativity; I was channeling it into something sustainable. That's something I think anyone starting a new project—whether it's a business or even just redecorating a home—should keep in mind. If you're trying to design your living space, don't feel pressure to follow every trend. Start with what you already love: a favorite color, a hand-me-down piece, something that makes you feel grounded. Build around that. If you're launching a new business, think about what skills or experiences you already have, what communities you're already part of, or even what your family history might offer. Sometimes the thing you've known your whole life—the thing you've overlooked because it seemed too obvious—is actually the key to something lasting and meaningful. You don't have to reinvent the wheel to build something beautiful. Often, the foundation you're looking for is already under your feet—you just have to stop long enough to notice it.

Once Sherry and I had accepted this foundation, we were able to come up with more innovative ideas. When one of our mother's two-story furniture buildings was sitting vacant, we saw another chance to try something new. We launched our very first concept store: a $599 Sofa Store. Every single sofa in the building, no matter how it looked, was priced at $599. It was simple and bold—and it worked. That first year, we made $1 million in sales. It was a huge milestone for us.

Eventually, Sherry and her husband took over the flooring business completely, which freed me up to open another furniture store. I called it Gallery Interiors. That's right—after looking down on my parents' furniture business most of my young life, I now had three.

Honoring where you come from doesn't mean you have to do things exactly the same way as those before you did. Embracing the core of my family business—the furniture itself—was a return to my roots, but I also knew I had to adapt if I wanted to thrive. Carrying out my parents' legacy meant a lot to me, but I never wanted to run the business the way they had. They relied on recourse credit—meaning if a customer defaulted, they were personally responsible to the bank. That kind of risk weighed heavily on my mother, and it was one of the reasons she'd grown to resent the business. Times had changed, though. We began working with institutions like Citibank, using revolving credit lines that removed our liability. If the customer was approved, we got paid—no strings attached. That shift allowed us to operate in a completely different mindset, one free of the stress and bitterness that had hung over the previous generation.

And guess what: It turned out running a furniture store could feel as creative and fulfilling as working with clothes. I had to do design work daily—staging and styling interiors across roughly 50,000 square feet of showroom space. The buildings weren't open concept or easy to navigate; they were older structures that had been stitched together over time. That made visual merchandising both a constant challenge and a source of inspiration.

• • •

I've said I wasn't expecting to ever get married. But I hadn't sworn off the possibility either. Then one day, a boy from town I'd known most of my life—a man now—dropped on my doorstep. I'm not kidding: I was living with a roommate at the time, and we were just watching a movie when this guy knocked on our door and asked to come in and hang out. I didn't know if someone had put him to it or what, but we settled into easy conversation, by the end of which he'd asked me out on a date. He was charming, and I accepted.

Flash forward six months, and he asked me to marry him. If that seems fast to you, well, you're right, it was. I agreed because, deep down, I think I was succumbing to a certain small-town pressure to conform. I'd always been an odd bird—wearing flashy outfits, driving around in flashy cars to run stores while playing hooky—and I liked that about myself. But when you're twenty-eight and one of the only unmarried women around, it's hard not to feel a bit bad.

On my wedding day, I stood arm in arm with my dad at the back of the church. There were four hundred people out there waiting. My dad, clearly sensing my hesitation, looked at me and said, "Paula, we can go out that front door right now. We don't have to walk down that aisle." He could tell I didn't want to go through with it. I told him it was just cold feet and that I couldn't disappoint all those people. He said, "You're only going to disappoint yourself if this isn't right." But I went through with it anyway.

The marriage lasted three and a half years. It turned out we simply weren't meant to be. But the ways in which I'd redrawn my life to suit our relationship had a profound and lasting effect. We'd agreed I would close Gallery Interiors, the only store I was running by then, because we could live off his salary, and because we expected me to become a mom soon. Truthfully, I could already see the cracks in the relationship and agreed to both—closing my business and becoming a stay-at-home mom—to help the marriage. But what this meant was that by the time we got divorced, I had no income and no business. I had sold off the inventory, shut the doors, and walked away from everything I had built.

So there I was: in my early thirties, divorced, and starting over.

It was one of the first real lessons I would learn about how your private life—marriage and motherhood or, in this case, simply the potential of motherhood—can have a significant impact on the life you lead publicly—in this case, my business. There would be many more lessons like this, some with much more dire consequences, along the way.

Business advice is often proffered in a vacuum, separate from people's messy inner lives. But I've come to see how being a woman, and the expectations that come along with that, inevitably shapes everything else, including your professional life. I'd closed down my business for the sake of the relationship, and now I was flat out of luck and money. I had to recalibrate everything—emotionally, financially, logistically.

On top of that, getting divorced in a small Bible Belt town is not easy. People talk, and talk gets nasty. I had to grow thick skin to get through it, and get creative about how to land back on my feet financially.

Here's what I want to say to you: Don't sacrifice your identity or your livelihood based on what you think others expect from you. I walked down that aisle because I didn't want to disappoint four hundred people, and I closed my business because I thought that's what a good wife would do. I should have listened to those warning signals, the voice inside my head telling me something was not right. Your intuition is smarter than you think. And it's important to keep one hand firmly on the wheel of your own life, especially during major transitions. Things like marriage, parenthood, or relocating can feel like they require total surrender, but they don't. Hold on to what makes you you—whether that's your business, your creative outlets, or your independence. It's not selfishness. It's self-preservation.

1. **You don't have to invent something new—you just have to look around.** For anyone out there trying to start something new—whether it's a business, a creative project, or even a new chapter in your life—I want to tell you this: You don't always have to go searching far and wide for your next big idea. Designing leather outfits for glamorous stars was only one way to be creative and independent. When I came back home and took a second look at the world I'd grown up in—my parents' furniture store, the small-town customer base, the hands-on business model—I realized there was something for me there too, and it didn't have to be forever. Don't overlook what you already know just because it feels too obvious. Sometimes the very thing you've taken for granted—your family's trade, a skill you've honed without thinking, the town you live in—is actually your calling, or just good enough for now.
2. **What seems "too simple" can actually be the smartest move.** We get told all the time that success comes from

innovation, from thinking outside the box, from making a big splash. And yes, sometimes that's true. But I've found again and again that some of my best business decisions have come from ideas so simple they almost felt silly. Our $599 Sofa Store is the perfect example. We priced every single sofa the same—$599—and that was it. No fancy marketing jargon, no tiered pricing system. Just one clear message. And customers loved it. They didn't have to guess or haggle or do mental math. So if you're stuck or overthinking something, ask yourself: Is there a simpler way? Often, cutting through the noise is the most effective thing you can do.

3. **Don't build your future on someone else's blueprint.** When I got married, I let go of a lot more than I realized. I closed my business because we'd agreed we could live off his income and that I'd become a stay-at-home mom. And even though I could already feel the cracks in the relationship, I convinced myself it was the right thing to do. Looking back, I see how much of that decision came from trying to fit into a version of life I thought I was supposed to want. But when the marriage ended, I didn't just lose a husband—I lost my business, my income, and the momentum I'd spent years building. So here's what I'll say to you, especially if you're navigating love or partnership while chasing your own dreams: Don't hand over your steering wheel. Stay true to yourself, and make sure you always have something solid to stand on.

CHAPTER 4

Back to the Drawing Board

Getting divorced was difficult, but I hardly had any time to feel bad about it. I had to make some cash, and make it fast. And I couldn't rely on the business that had sustained me for the last few years, because I'd recently sold it. So I came up with what seemed like a harebrained scheme at the time.

For years, I'd been attending High Point Market (then called the International Home Furnishings Market) in High Point, North Carolina—the biggest home furnishing trade show in the world. Instead of just going as a buyer for the upcoming Spring Market that year, I decided I would lease showroom space and then sublet it to vendors selling handmade items. Basically, I'd be a landlord for five days and pocket the difference.

I got on the phone and started making calls. Someone at the Commerce & Design Building told me they had an entire showroom sitting empty on the bottom floor. I jumped at the opportunity, borrowed money from my parents, and signed the lease.

The showroom had twenty spaces. Within days, I'd rented out every space except for one corner in the back. I decided to keep that one for myself. I figured I'd be at the show anyway, and this space wasn't costing me anything. Why not make a little extra by selling something myself? The only question was: What?

There was a store in Knoxville that sold unfinished white plaster decorative items—statues, busts, columns, candleholders, and the like. One day, as I browsed the aisles, it struck me that the candleholders had potential. Nothing revolutionary, but I could see possibilities.

I bought a load of candleholders in various shapes and sizes, drove back to Oneida, and turned my dad's barn into an impromptu workshop. I stayed up all night painting and decorating the candleholders. When I finished, I had about forty to fifty high-end-looking candleholders you'd have never guessed started as basic plaster. My favorite was shaped like the letter "U" and reminded me of Noah's ark. I dressed it up with a floral arrangement at the base and topped it with elegant white and gold candles. I took them to High Point and set them up in my corner space with strategic lighting and floral accents. And guess what: My candles sold like hotcakes.

There was a rumor flying around the market that two Saudi princes who owned American Home Furnishings were on the hunt for items to buy. One of my renters dropped by to tell me as much but assured me the princes would have no interest in my stall. "Trust me, they'll never buy from you. They don't purchase from a company unless they've seen them at market for at least two or three years," he said. But when the princes dropped by my corner, they ordered multiples of everything I had to the tune of $44,000. That was on top of the $7,000–$8,000 worth of smaller orders that people had placed at the show.

I was gripped by a familiar feeling of jubilance mixed with confusion. *What the hell?* I'd gotten myself a space at High Point to make a few bucks on the side. Now, all of a sudden, I had a real product line and a business to run—but no manufacturing capacity to fill such a massive order.

In business as in life, I was going back to the drawing board. I was newly single and now, suddenly, the head of a manufacturing business I had to scale up—and fast.

I started with the space. My father's barn was large but cluttered with farm equipment and years of accumulated stuff. I spent three full days clearing out half the barn, setting up proper workbenches, and installing enough lighting so we could work into the night if needed.

Next came the challenge of hiring people. In Oneida, jobs were scarce, but finding people with artistic ability was even harder. I started with three local women who had some craft experience. I learned to make molds and cast them myself. Instead of buying premade plaster pieces, I started pouring my own. It was a steep learning curve—figuring out the right plaster consistency, drying times, and how to prevent air bubbles. I developed a production system where each person had specific responsibilities. One person would prepare the plaster pieces, another would apply the base coat, and another would add the decorative elements. I did all the final detailing myself to ensure consistency. We worked twelve-hour days trying to meet our deadline.

The first shipment to the Saudi brothers was a nail-biter. When they called to say they were thrilled with the products and wanted to place another order, I realized I was in deep.

Before long, my products had gotten attention and were displayed in showrooms ranging from the Boxer Collection and Gregory Gallery in New York City to the Dallas Market Center and Chicago Showroom. Within six months, I had expanded to fourteen employees and taken over the entire barn. We were producing thousands of pieces monthly. Each new showroom opened doors to others.

I'd successfully reinvented myself in the wake of my divorce, and I was proud of that, even if the work was exhausting and occasionally overwhelming.

Maintaining a permanent space at High Point was prohibitively expensive, so every market, I'd take temporary booth space, haul all my products down there, and spend a week setting up displays. It was just hard work—bust-your-ass work—making my space look perfect every six months, then tearing it all down again.

Also, my pieces were literally breaking. It turns out there are some serious limitations with plaster. First, it's extremely fragile. The pieces often broke during shipping, and I had to replace them at my expense. Second, plaster pieces are typically sold as individual items, not collections, which limited how much I could grow my business.

So I decided to pivot to decoupage—cutting designs from paper, applying them to wooden objects, and coating everything with varnish. Suddenly I could create entire collections of matching items: wooden tissue boxes, wastebaskets, small decorative boxes, mirrors, wall décor, and shelves. And wooden items rarely broke during shipping, solving my biggest headache.

I threw myself into experimenting with different papers and techniques. I developed a special antiquing solution using paint and Vaseline that gave the paper an aged appearance and created a beautiful finish. I called this new collection "Accent Originals."

I made one original piece of art for whatever product I was working on at the time—wastebaskets, tissue covers, calcium carbonate figurines, you name it. We poured and cast these figurines—dogs, busts, and all kinds of beautiful home accessories—then gold-leafed them and applied faux finishes.

I'd create the original, put it into the line, and then my team would duplicate it. They sold exceptionally well. Those waste-baskets went for $98 each, which seemed exorbitant at the time, but people like Sylvester Stallone, Joan Collins, and other entertainers bought them because they were gorgeous.

Accent Originals was so successful, and selling at such a high price point, I thought, you know what? I'm going to make a lower price point of these items. I called that line "Sassy."

The last High Point Market I attended, I'd finally turned a profit after years of reinvesting everything back into the business. That's when a buyer from Service Merchandise walked through my booth and placed a $1 million purchase order for my Sassy line.

I stood there looking at this piece of paper that was simultaneously worth a fortune and completely worthless to me. I didn't even have enough money to fund the raw materials for this order. I had no idea how I would fulfill it. I didn't understand their requirements for Electronic Data Interchange (EDI) ordering, barcodes, shipping logistics—it was all new to me. I desperately wanted to do it, but I had no idea how.

Word traveled around High Point almost as fast as it did in Oneida: Soon, everybody was talking about this little Tennessee company that had landed a million-dollar order.

Then one day, some guy who was also working as a vendor in the show dropped by. He and his family, the Lawrences, were pretty wealthy folks who were buying up small companies because they needed to diversify their fortune. Their main business was making antennas for cars, but antennas wouldn't be on cars much longer. He explained that they were buying furniture companies. And they were interested in buying my Sassy line.

Since I'd received the order, I'd been trying to get funding to fill it. I turned to my local community, thinking I could tap into federal funding that had been set aside for small businesses in our underserved area. Turns out they'd been given millions to support entrepreneurs like me, but they wouldn't lift a finger unless I agreed to bring them in as partners. It was all backroom deals—local men controlling the money, trying to slide in and get ownership in exchange for access. I didn't know that game. I wasn't part of those conversations, didn't understand how that under-the-table stuff worked. And because I wasn't willing to play it their way, they shut me out.

The Lawrences were offering to use my million-dollar purchase order as the catalyst to start a business with me. They just wanted to know one thing. How would I feel about moving to Cleveland?

I didn't think twice. I was ready.

First of all, I was over my skis at that point running the manufacturing business on my own. I knew I needed more help than what was available to me in Oneida. I needed solid accounting help, more structure—things that town didn't really offer. It's small, and while there were plenty of blue-collar workers, white-collar talent was hard to come by. And honestly, drugs were everywhere back then. People would show up on Mondays sick as dogs from partying all weekend—throwing up, hungover. Especially the creatives—the ones who were supposed to be translating my designs. I'd make the original, and they'd replicate it, but most of them were out of it half the time. High as hell—smoking, popping pills. I had to put them on piecework just to get anything done, because otherwise I'd look out and they'd be passed out on the tables, trying to sober up.

Plus, I saw working with the Lawrences and moving to Cleveland as the be-all, end-all escape from Oneida I'd been hoping for and planning since I was a kid. While I had left before when I went on tour, as long as my parents were alive, I still always had one foot in town. My mother had lived her life for me, and I knew if I ever "really" left, she would have been devastated. My brother's words still rang in my head: "You're a big fish in a little pond, girly." Now, at last, was my chance to swim out to open waters.

I accepted the Lawrences' offer. They told me to keep all the money from the orders I'd made at the show, put it in my pocket, and just pack up and come to Cleveland. And that's what I was about to do. A clean break.

The next few months were a flurry of preparations boxing up the business—and my life—in Oneida.

The Lawrences found me a place to live in Chagrin Falls. They were excited about me making the move, and incredibly helpful. They also made sure I was as excited as they were, and available. They asked me if I had any plans to get married or have children any time soon. My answer was a resounding no.

The Lawrences were starting to feel like family. They didn't have any daughters, only three sons, and we were growing close. I'd gone to Cleveland and toured their factories, gone to their homes, and spent a couple of days with them. They were good, solid people to be in business with. My parents, although they were sad to see me go, agreed and felt good about it too.

I can't tell you how excited I was about this new opportunity. Finally, I would be able to focus solely on design without having to wear all the hats—manufacturing, packaging, sales, accounting. They had the business infrastructure, the funding, and the expertise to handle everything else. *I'm going to have a legitimate business*, I thought. These people saw my value, and they had the business construct. All I had to do was get myself up to Cleveland, and they would help me with all the other facets of the business they already knew how to maneuver. They had money to fund it, and it was all going to be amazing.

I was driving back from Cleveland after finalizing arrangements with the Lawrences, crossing the bridge into Louisville,

Kentucky—ironically, the city I would eventually return to—when suddenly, I felt horribly ill and had to pull over.

When the nausea wouldn't go away, I went to the pharmacy and got a test. You may have guessed it. I was pregnant.

How on earth, you're asking? I wondered the same.

Well, we knew each other from high school, but only really as acquaintances. He'd dropped by the manufacturing shop to talk to one of my employees one day and seen that I was closing things down, trying to fulfill my last orders and hold it all together. Next thing I knew, he was helping me after hours, boxing things up, just all around being useful. I appreciated it, because I was letting go of most of my crew by then.

We got along, and he asked if I'd help him with some ideas redecorating his house. It was clear we liked each other. I thought, *Why not? Why not have a quick fling?* I was moving—what could go wrong if I dated this nice man from my hometown during the short amount of time I had left in it?

Well, I found out exactly what could go wrong. I was stunned by the pregnancy, and so was he. But we both agreed marriage was not in our stars. "I just want to have this baby," I told him. "You don't owe me anything. You do you, and I'll do me. Let's just stay friends."

And ultimately, that's what we did. We stayed friends and raised our son without the mess that could have come along with this kind of situation. Thankfully, there was no fighting, no court battles, no drama.

But I'm getting ahead of myself. At that moment in time, I had a gigantic decision to make. Could I still go through with the Cleveland move? I'd gone back to the drawing board and pulled myself out of the depths of my divorce. I was solvent. More than solvent—I was successful. But now I had to face another hurdle, one that many women have, sometime or another. Could I pursue my professional dream with, unexpectedly, a baby on the way?

Getting pregnant would send me back to that drawing board again, and though it felt like I was stepping off the path of success at the time, it would ultimately bring me a little closer to my dreams. But I still had to learn that.

1. **Sometimes reinvention isn't a choice—it's survival.** After my divorce, I didn't just lose a marriage—I lost the business I'd relied on for my livelihood as well. I had to start from scratch, and fast. That's what pushed me to buy and lease space at High Point, and what got me into manufacturing. It wasn't because I had a grand vision, but because I had to get going again. I didn't know how to cast plaster or run a production line—I figured it out because I had to. Sometimes what you need most is to feel in control—even if it's not the kind of control you pictured. You might've imagined designing in a studio, not hauling buckets of plaster and pulling all-nighters. But control isn't always glamorous—it's about knowing the work is getting done, because you figured out how to do it.
2. **Don't toss out your creativity—repackage it.** When I created my Sassy line, it wasn't some brand-new concept. It was my own designs, just reimagined in a more affordable, scalable way. The fancy Accent Originals line proved the concept worked—but Sassy made it

accessible. And that "knockoff" of my own work? It got a $1 million order. The truth is, you don't always need a new idea—sometimes you need a new way to deliver the idea. If something works, don't be afraid to strip it down, simplify it, and serve it to a different audience. Accessibility doesn't cheapen creativity.

3. **Some of life's biggest blessings start as "back to the drawing board" moments.** First it was my divorce—everything I'd built got tied up and sold off, and I had to start over from scratch. Then, just when I thought I had my future mapped out again—a move to Cleveland, a million-dollar order, a fresh start—I found out I was pregnant. It felt like the rug got pulled out from under me all over again. But here's what I've learned: Those moments that feel like setbacks can be the beginning of something more meaningful. My son would become the most treasured part of my life. What I feared would derail my dreams ended up grounding me in a much deeper purpose. So don't be afraid of going back to the drawing board. Sometimes that's where life sketches out its most beautiful surprises.

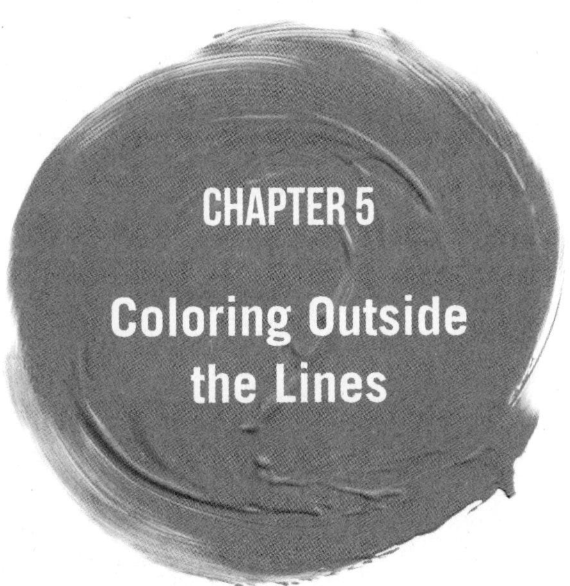

CHAPTER 5

Coloring Outside the Lines

I wasn't a child when I got pregnant. I was thirty-two. An old gal by Oneida's standards.

I had to muster all my courage to tell my parents. I told my mother first. She was hurt because I wasn't even in a relationship with the father, much less married to him. But she accepted it. My mother always supported me.

My whole life, information had gone from my mother to my father, but this time she said to me, "I'm going to let you tell your father first."

"I'm not proud to tell you this, but I'm having a baby," I told my dad. He sat there for a minute in silence. And then he said, "Well, all I can say is this. If you can take it, I can take it. But you can't go to Cleveland." I looked at him, and he continued. "I'm sorry. You don't know a soul there, and you've never had a baby. I've had several and I know what it's like, how much work it is."

I told him I'd figure it out. He said he'd build a crib in his house, and his house only, and that that's where I should go. My mother agreed. Neither of them ever saw me having a baby, and they didn't think I could do it on my own. I protested, but, in the end, that's what I did.

Imagine that: I hadn't lived with my parents since I was eighteen. If this is a book about what to do when you feel stuck, at that point in my life, I felt more than stuck—I felt like I'd gone back in time.

Being pregnant was a brokenhearted kind of joy, for me and for my parents. None of us could have prepared for it. My mom and my dad could see how much heartache I carried because, I felt, there was no righting the wrong of having a child out of wedlock. It was something I would have to carry for the rest of my days. And it wasn't just my cross to bear, but it was my son's as well. How would I make him feel like he hadn't been rejected by his father? How would I shield him from the judgment that would inevitably come our way in a small town like Oneida?

You have to remember, we were living in the Bible Belt. People acted as if they had a license to judge you. If you sinned, you'd better do it in private. That's why most people didn't drink in public—they'd drive over to Knoxville to do it. As long as appearances were maintained, you were in the clear. But I couldn't exactly hide my pregnancy or my child, nor did I want to. And so I was branded with a giant scarlet letter, and not the kind sewed onto a cute leather jacket I would have wanted to wear.

If I thought the gossip after my divorce was bad, I braced myself for what it would be like now. I didn't want my son to experience that stigma. He hadn't done anything to deserve it.

After I had the baby, my dad was the first person who came by the hospital. I was propped up on the bed, holding my son, my Brady, in my arms. My dad didn't say anything, he just grabbed my foot and gently pinched my toe. My mother relished being a grandmother and became completely focused on the baby. She hadn't been able to be completely focused on my sister and me when we were growing up because she was busy growing her business, something I used to resent, but she could be present now.

Having a baby on my own, clear-eyed about what that meant and would mean for our future, is probably the hardest thing I've ever done. It was also the best mistake of my life.

• • •

That didn't make breaking the news to the Lawrences any easier, though. When I'd first met them at High Point, they'd wanted to make sure I didn't have any personal "entanglements" that might interfere with our business arrangement. I'd assured them I didn't. "I'm creating, designing, and packaging boxes; I'm wearing all the hats and managing a team of employees. My head's buried in the business—I'm simply too busy to date anyone," I'd told them. And I'd been honest. Sometime after finding out I was pregnant, I broke the news to the Lawrences and told them I couldn't go through with our arrangement. I admit I could have handled it better. I was overwhelmed with emotion and couldn't bring myself to tell them the whole story. I simply informed them I wouldn't be coming to Cleveland, offering little explanation. It wasn't my proudest moment.

Luckily, they hadn't invested any money in the business yet. There was no financial insult to add to the injury of my news. Years later, I reached out to apologize and thank them for the encouragement they'd given me. They were supportive and gracious, and for that I am grateful.

So for now, my great escape from Oneida was on hold. It was time to hunker down and find stability. I had a baby to care for.

I found myself taking inventory of what I had—and what I didn't. I didn't have a formal education to rely on. There was no business degree hanging on a wall. What I did have was my creativity. It was time to open another jar, but this time, not just for my sake.

Having Brady changed everything. Suddenly, I had this tiny human whose needs came before my own. I understood how Sherry must have felt when she had her first child, when suddenly she'd lost interest in clothes and fashion. Having a baby recalibrated my compass. And as a single parent, the weight of responsibility sat heavy and real on my shoulders—providing food, shelter, education, and love. Making money was no longer at the service of funding my escape from Oneida. Now it was all about creating stability for my son.

I'd never shied away from the unconventional. I was the girl who rocked bold suede shoes when everyone else wore sneakers, who ditched school to run a clothing store, who held off on getting married because she was busy touring with Tanya Tucker. I had no problem with that. I was comfortable being flashy. Having a child on my own was a whole different can of worms, however. It was another way I didn't fit the mold, but it came with a more affecting kind of moral judgment from people in town.

I'd colored outside the lines of convention. I had to accept it, even when it got hard.

Most children enter this world unplanned. Mine certainly did, and he didn't arrive with what Oneida might call proper circumstances. But I committed to raising a remarkable human, to aim him toward possibilities I hadn't imagined for myself.

Having Brady forced me to reconsider everything about my approach to life and business. Before him, I was always chasing the next big opportunity, always eyeing the exit from small-town life. After him, I built for security, stability, and something that would last beyond me.

In business, as in raising a child, your plans will collapse. What matters isn't how meticulously you plot your course but your ability to adapt when circumstances change. Brady sharpened my focus. He gave me a clear purpose. Ultimately, he would give me the courage to open some jars I might otherwise never have opened.

• • •

But in the present moment, it was time to find a way to earn a living. There was no way I could return to the manufacturing business. Even though I'd finally turned a profit and secured that million-dollar order, the materials weren't safe around a newborn, and the demanding hours didn't work for me as a new mom.

Just like I'd known it was time to walk away from touring with Tanya back in my leather design days, I recognized the signs here too. It was time to move on.

With my manufacturing business closed and my Cleveland plans shelved, I needed a new business strategy that suited my time and energy levels as a new mom. Brady was tiny; I was still breastfeeding him. Then I had an idea. I'd noticed how traffic patterns in Oneida had changed, and how most traffic was no longer concentrated in the center of town around Main Avenue but was instead farther up the thoroughfare along Highway 27.

I found a little building close to the highway with two big, beautiful windows directly facing the road. Instant advertising. I just needed to fill those displays with head-turning items. I did, and called the store "Romantique."

I dressed those windows up to look like something you'd see on Fifth Avenue in New York City—lavish, eye-catching displays that would make cars slow down as they passed. One window I remember particularly well featured beautiful lamp figures I'd painted and decorated. I made all the lampshades out of old straw hats and women's hats, decorating them with ribbons and flowers. I even created fake rain coming down in the display. It was whimsical, unique—a little piece of artistry in our small town.

Around this time, my dad's sister, his only sister who had no children of her own, moved in with me and helped care for Brady. Her companionship was a godsend. Together, we spent our days creating one-of-a-kind original pieces. I'd scour the area for old music boxes, trinkets, lamps, chairs, tables—anything with potential. Then, like my mother had done with those secondhand baby cribs, I'd transform them into elaborate art pieces. And just as she'd set up a craft space for Sherry and me, I put a nursery in the back of the store where Brady could sleep while I worked.

The window displays worked: Drivers pulled over and dropped in, intrigued. I'd make $1,000 a day in sales just selling those little trinkets I'd made. For a small business in Oneida, that was pretty remarkable. I'd realized that my store was strategically located on the route to Kentucky. This meant I got customers who were just passing through—people who didn't live in town and could pay higher prices than locals.

• • •

Then, around the time Brady turned two, I switched gears and started helping my dad out with the furniture store. Yep, I was back in the old family business. My mom was still busy taking care of my grandmother, who wasn't doing too well, which left my father running their store alone—and struggling, big time.

In my mom's absence, the place had gone from the homey space where customers caught up while browsing her beautiful refurbished pieces to a dilapidated mess, with leaky roofs and merchandise covered in plastic. Dad called it a "museum" because nobody bought anything anymore. They just walked through, looked, and left. When I saw the state of things, I couldn't believe it. "Oh my God, Dad," I said. "There's no lights on in here. It's practically raining in the building."

My dad at first wasn't thrilled about me joining the business. He'd gotten comfortable sitting around with his friends most of the day, talking and keeping warm by the woodstove. Now here I was, kicking his behind and telling him we needed to clean the place up, turn on the gas heat, and actually run it like a business.

Now that I held the reins, I could do things my way. First, I transformed the inventory. Everything had been sitting there for years, covered in plastic like ancient artifacts in a dusty museum. Dad insisted none of it would sell. "Well, you can't sell it with plastic over it," I told him. I cleaned everything up, turned on the lights, fixed the roof leaks, and started working on the cosmetics of the building—painting it, lighting it properly, making it look like a store instead of somebody's old attic.

One building we owned was a mammoth—300 feet long by 75 feet wide—completely filled with old merchandise and junk that had accumulated over decades. It was like an archaeological dig through my family's business history, with layers representing different eras: my grandparents' ventures, my parents' early attempts, newer stock that had never seen the showroom floor. It took me a year and a half, with several men working alongside me, to empty that building completely—hauling, dumping, burning, whatever it took. My sister still uses that building today.

Working with my dad was the partnership I needed at the time. We whipped the store back into shape, and I got help with Brady, who was now a toddler—a sweet handful.

Just as Brady was growing up, Oneida was changing too. And in that chance, I spotted another opportunity.

Wealthy folks from Gatlinburg, Tennessee, began buying land and building second homes in Oneida. They were people who'd made their fortunes in the tourism trade of the Smoky Mountains but now felt squeezed out of their own towns. Gatlinburg and Pigeon Forge had transformed from peaceful mountain retreats into congested tourist traps full of miniature golf courses and souvenir shops.

These folks were looking for the natural beauty they once loved about Gatlinburg—before it became overrun with attractions. Oneida, built along the Big South Fork River and Recreation Area, offered exactly that. It was a federal park with breathtaking scenery, trails, water, and wildlife—they'd reintroduced elk, eagles, and bear to the area. But the best part? Almost no one knew about it. It was just a ninety-minute drive from Gatlinburg but felt worlds away in terms of serenity.

So these people came to Oneida and built second homes, seeking the peace they'd lost. And they didn't want the hassle of furnishing these places themselves. They wanted someone to handle everything—put sheets on the beds, dishes in the cupboards, art on the walls, the works. They wanted to be able to walk in with nothing but groceries and immediately start living there.

And that's how I stumbled into my first real opportunity as an interior designer. I ended up furnishing nearly every single cabin built in that area during that period. It was more than decorating; it was creating turnkey retreats where these people could escape and reconnect with nature. And I was never once asked to show a diploma, proving my long-ago hunch that I didn't need a degree in design to do good work.

To complement that work, I opened another furniture store with items this crowd of newcomers would want for their new homes. I called it BT Trading Company after my son, Braden Terry. My shop looked like something straight out of an old Western movie. It had that classic frontier storefront—logs across the facade and a big king post right on the front. It was eye-catching and distinctive, not your typical retail space.

That's where I was when a millionaire walked in.

1. **You don't have to apologize to the world for the unconventional turns in your own life.** I'd never fit neatly into Oneida's boxes, but nothing brought judgment like being pregnant and unmarried in the Bible Belt. I knew I was fueling the rumor mill with a pregnancy I couldn't hide. I also knew my son had done nothing wrong and deserved none of those whispers. So I made a decision. I refused to apologize for my son's existence. Whatever mistakes I'd made had nothing to do with him. The moment you start defending yourself against other people's judgment is the moment you give it power. Instead, I chose to live openly and build a life where Brady and I could thrive regardless of what anyone thought. I encourage you to do the same: Live your own life, and don't worry about the noise.
2. **What looks like your biggest constraint may become your greatest blessing.** When I found out I was pregnant, it felt like the universe had thrown up a massive roadblock in

my path. Cleveland was off the table. Manufacturing was suddenly impossible with its toxic materials and grueling hours. My great escape from Oneida was postponed indefinitely. But here's the truth I didn't see coming: Brady forced me to slow down in ways nothing else could have. I put a nursery in the back of my shop so I could watch him while I worked. I designed window displays that would catch eyes while I nursed him. I structured my entire business around being present for his first smile, first steps, first words—moments I might have missed if I was swamped by work in Cleveland. Sometimes in business, it's important to take a beat to appreciate what really matters.

3. **Your portfolio speaks louder than any degree.** Interior design became the perfect vehicle to showcase every skill I'd accumulated throughout my wandering career path. All those years watching my mom transform secondhand furniture, my obsession with colors from my clothing stores, the aesthetic sense I'd developed designing for country stars—it all converged in this new venture. And not a single client asked where I went to design school or what credentials I had. They saw my work, they loved it, they hired me. I didn't have an interior design degree, but I did have a lifetime of hands-on experience and an eye that no classroom could teach. I knew how to walk into a room, immediately see its potential, and bring that vision to life within any budget. In creative fields especially, your portfolio will always speak volumes more than framed credentials.

CHAPTER 6

When Paint Peels Back

It was a regular Tuesday afternoon when an odd pair walked into BT Trading.

He had black, slicked-back hair, white shoes, a wife-beater tank top over jeans, and a small ram tattoo on his arm. He didn't look like anyone around Oneida. His fiancée was even more conspicuous in her hot-pink Juicy Couture outfit, platform high heels, and Hello Kitty purse, with blonde hair that seemed to go on forever.

We started talking, and I learned his name was Glenn Nelson and that he'd bought Jim Barna's old house at auction. Barna was a Hungarian immigrant who had built one of the largest log home manufacturing businesses in the country. I'd decorated all his model homes over the years, including the one he lived in. Everyone in town had been curious about the New Yorker who'd bought the place but never showed up. And now here he was, standing in front of me.

"Hey, would you be interested in working for me and furnishing my house?" Glenn asked.

"Sure," I answered. "How quickly do you want it done?"

"We're here for two days," he said.

"So you mean right now?" I asked.

"Yeah," he answered.

That same day, we loaded about $35,000 worth of furniture into trucks and set it all up in Glenn's new house. It was nearly midnight by the time we were done. As a final, finishing touch, I put two large terra-cotta olive jars in the entryway. I thought they were perfect for a rustic but grandiose home like his. Before I left, his fiancée discreetly motioned me to not give Glenn the bill, and took me aside to handle the transaction herself. I understood why soon.

Five days later, Glenn showed up at my store, absolutely livid. He thrust the bill at me, steam practically coming out of his ears. "I've never seen a vase worth this amount of money!" he shouted, referring to the olive jars. "Get those goddamn vases out of my goddamn house and take them off my bill!"

I was stunned. Not just by his rudeness, but because I'd already given him a huge discount on those jars, charging $400 for the pair when they retailed for about twice that. But I could see reasoning with him would be pointless. I cut the price to $200, thinking, "Once I collect on this bill, I'm never doing business with this guy again."

He scribbled out a check, tossed it at me, and left. I thought that'd be the end of my dealings with this eccentric

New Yorker. But just a few days later, he emailed asking me to install a Ping-Pong table, pool table, and television in his game room. When I asked about the budget to make sure I avoided another meltdown, he answered, "There is no budget." This time, he didn't complain about the bill when I sent it.

A few weeks after that, he returned and asked if I'd be interested in working on a building of his in Cleveland. "What kind of building is it?" I asked. "A fifteen-story high-rise," he answered casually. I figured he was exaggerating. Sure, he'd spent a decent amount of money on Jim Barna's old place, but he drove around in a high-top minivan that didn't exactly scream "successful businessman."

It was only when I got to walk through this massive building with Glenn and his team of suits—Harvard and Yale graduates who looked at me, this small-town Tennessee decorator, like I'd dropped in from another planet—that it finally sunk in that I was dealing with a multimillionaire.

As we toured the building, Glenn asked his crew what they would do with various spaces. Their answers were consistently expensive and elaborate. "We'd tear out all these toilets and walls, and start fresh," they'd insist. Or, "We'd re-stainless steel these elevators, put in new mahogany, new marble floors."

When Glenn turned to me and asked what I would do, I said, "I'd paint. I wouldn't tear any of that out. I'd just paint over." I could tell he was intrigued. At the end of the day, Glenn looked at me and said, "I like you. You know why? You know how to put fucking lipstick on a pig."

What I realized later was that Glenn was surrounded by yes-men who told him what they thought he wanted to hear. I was the only one who argued with him, who told him what I didn't necessarily think he wanted to hear. And that's exactly what he needed.

And that was the beginning of a yearslong working relationship with Glenn, an impetuous but wildly successful multimillionaire.

We had a complicated love-hate relationship. I'd be lying if I said working with him was easy. He could be a complete nightmare. But the truth is, that man taught me more in six years than I could have learned in twenty at some fancy business school. He was an entrepreneur who took massive risks. He bought a 2.5-million-square-foot building in Danbury, Connecticut, for $256 million when the economy was still shaky from the 2008 financial crisis, aiming to lease space to Fortune 500 companies hoping to escape New York taxes. It was the largest purchase of a commercial building from a corporate entity like Grubb & Ellis ever to go back into the hands of a single owner. Glenn renovated it and attracted Class A tenants like PepsiCo, General Motors, and other Fortune 500 companies. And I got to design all those spaces.

Working with graduate-degree designers who did everything by the book meant I had to learn the terminology and methods they used. I'd always worked by instinct; I didn't speak their language. But there was value to learning it.

Working with Glenn could be tough. He was unpredictable and demanding. Honestly, sometimes I felt like he was giving me an important lesson in what not to do as a business owner.

But Glenn respected me because I stood my ground. I saw how he operated, how he made decisions, how he took big risks and sometimes won big. My base salary wasn't impressive, but I made it work by becoming his supplier for furniture and materials used in the redecorating jobs. I'd create my own price lists, ensure they were competitive, and take a healthy cut of everything I sold him. So despite the constant battles, I did very well financially during those years.

I was absorbing it all, filing it away for my own future.

Looking back, I see that Glenn and Tanya Tucker were similar in many ways. Each was the sun in their own solar system, with planets—people like me—revolving around them. Both opened doors for me I couldn't have opened for myself. But I didn't belong in their worlds and didn't want to. There was too much artifice; that much money and power could make it all feel too much like a circus. And in Glenn's case, I could see how much it hurt his relationships.

It's trite to say but true. Money doesn't buy happiness. It doesn't buy family or friends. If anything, it can create distance from those things. It can unravel your healthy relationships with family, and dissolve friendships in ways you can't control. Once people see you at that level—once they recognize your monetary success—they change how they look at you. Then you don't know what's real and what's not. Your discernment suffers, and you can't see through people's intentions. You constantly wonder: *What do they want from me?* Even worse is when you start hanging that suspicion on everyone. That's what I saw happen to Glenn: His wealth made him cynical and closed him off to people. It's an obvious but important lesson.

Working with Glenn taught me a lot, but it also revealed a hard truth. When paint peels back, you see what's underneath. On the surface, Glenn's life looked shiny: money, power, prestige. But the deeper I got, the more I saw the cracks. The way people drifted from him or were pushed out. That peeling back didn't just show me who he was—it forced me to look at my own life too. What was hiding beneath my surface? What had I covered up for too long?

Too much, it turned out.

• • •

While my professional life was reaching new heights, my personal life had descended into darkness. As a single mom living in Oneida with a young son, I found myself in a situation I had never anticipated. I was trapped in a relationship with a man who seemed determined to break me down. Brady was still practically a baby when we started dating and, at first, he seemed like everything I could want. Charming, attentive, and wonderful with Brady. I thought I'd found a father figure for my son.

I'm not going to dwell on the details. What I will say is this: When someone works systematically to erode your confidence, you start to believe them.

What makes abuse so insidious is how it creeps in slowly. It's rarely as dramatic as the stories we see on television. Instead, it's a slow and steady process by which you start to doubt your reality and your sense of self. It's being told over and over that you're worthless until you start to believe it. It's wondering if maybe you really are the problem. What made this all even harder was that Brady adored him. How do you explain to a young child that the man who plays with him in the yard is the same person causing his mother harm?

And here's the really messed up part: I loved him. Or at least I thought I did. Looking back, I kept telling myself, *If he just wouldn't be this brutal person sometimes, he could be so wonderful.*

That's the crazy-making part of these relationships—those moments of charm or kindness that keep you hanging on, hoping the monster will disappear and the nice guy will stay. But that's not how it works.

It affected my whole life. I lost interest in art—me, for whom creating had always been so fundamental. I just didn't see the point. And it also affected my work. Before I started working with Glenn, I'd worry about this man coming into my stores. I carried a level of stress around that I wouldn't wish on any human being.

At one point, I was *this* close to giving up—to actually believing I was worthless. That's how far gone I was. I'd started to think, *Well, maybe this is just my life now.*

But there was this stubborn little voice deep inside me that wouldn't shut up. *Fight*, it kept saying. *Keep going, girl. You've got to get away from this.*

Working for Glenn provided a small escape. The job meant traveling every other week to Connecticut, spending Monday through Thursday away from Brady, who stayed with a nanny in my absence. But I'd come home, and the situation would still be the same.

Getting out was one of the hardest things I've ever done. It took me years, during which I often felt deeply alone. People around me, townsfolk and even my family, didn't understand because they didn't see. Including my mom—even though long ago, before I was born, she'd been trapped in a similar situation.

She'd wanted to protect Sherry and me from this part of her life by not letting us know about it. But growing up in a small town, rumors have a way of finding you. Around the time I turned eighteen, I confronted her, and she explained that she had once been in a relationship with a violent man. Suddenly, a few things made sense. As a kid, I'd never gotten why some customers would get so emotional talking to my mom over simple furniture transactions. Why they were so loyal. It was because they knew her story; how much she'd suffered, and how much she'd overcome.

It was with somewhat of a sinking heart that I realized history was repeating itself with me. I had to get Brady and me out, and break the cycle.

• • •

Here's what I want to say to you. If you've been in this situation—if you are in it now—there is hope on the other side. As desperate as it feels, as lonely and isolated as you believe your pain is, or as impossible as escape seems—you can get out. There is help.

I'm talking about this in the context of my journey as a businesswoman because sometimes the biggest thing holding you back isn't your strategy or your funding or your competition. Sometimes it's what's happening behind closed doors when you go home at night. If that's you, please know you're not alone. And more importantly, know that you deserve better. You shouldn't feel like you're always walking on eggshells, constantly anxious, second-guessing your every move. You shouldn't lose the spark that drives your creativity, or your work. You shouldn't have to use up all your courage just to get through the day.

It took some time, but finally, my family—my parents and Sherry—started understanding what I was going through, and backing me up. And slowly, I escaped his hold. It was a psychological untethering at first. I started telling myself that the version of reality he was spinning just couldn't be true. And in time, I started actually believing it. After that, I could finally start imagining a physical escape: moving away from Oneida.

Besides, there were other reasons why I felt Brady and I had to get out. I wanted Brady to have more opportunities than Oneida could provide. You could only go so far there and I wanted him to escape small-town scrutiny. If I walked into a restaurant, I knew what half the people there would be whispering. "Oh, there's Paula. Her son's done kind of good." "Yeah, they've done all right. She's raised him, at least he's not a drug addict." At least most of it was somewhat positive. But I still didn't want that kind of talk to define Brady.

Because the thing is, I wouldn't change having Brady for anything in this world. My son is absolutely brilliant—off-the-chain smart—because he's a product of his father's intelligence and whatever genes I've contributed. I wouldn't change one piece of that. No way. No matter who's judging. I just didn't want his circumstances to taint his future. I didn't want people always knowing him as "that boy" whose mother wasn't married when she had him. He deserved to be known for who he is, not how he came into this world.

I made the decision to leave Oneida sometime in 2011. It took almost two more years before I could finally pull the trigger.

In 2009 my mom got sick and passed away quickly. My dad followed her not long after. It was devastating losing them both. It was also the final nudge I needed. One of the main reasons I'd stayed in Oneida all those years was for them. Because I loved them, but also because I knew they didn't want me to leave them. Now that they were gone, nothing tied me to that town anymore. I could finally get the hell out.

In 2013, Brady and I moved to Louisville, a city where no one knew our history, where Brady could attend a better school, and where we could build something new together. Where whispers couldn't follow us, especially him.

Finding my footing after getting divorced and having a kid as a single mom were tough jars to open, no doubt about it. But leaving Oneida for all the reasons I've explained was probably the toughest jar of all. In my professional life, I'd always been fearless—running headlong into new ventures, reinventing myself from retailer to designer to manufacturer without batting an eye. In my private life, when I was at my lowest, I struggled to even see a future. It's like I was two different people: a bold entrepreneur who could take on anyone in the business world—even someone like Glenn—and this other person I didn't recognize. If you feel a disconnect between who you know you are and who you've been reduced to, I want you to believe you can find a way back to yourself. This particular "open the jar" moment—my decision to pack up and start over in Louisville—felt impossible until I did it. And though I didn't know it at the time, that fresh start would ultimately lead directly to Heirloom Traditions Paint, the business that changed everything.

1. **Your greatest value can come from honest disagreement.** I learned that success sometimes means being the only one willing to say what others won't. When everyone in Glenn's entourage suggested expensive renovations, I simply said, "I'd paint." That honesty—being willing to argue with a millionaire when his yes-men wouldn't—became my greatest asset. Glenn respected me precisely because I stood my ground. In both business and personal relationships, don't sacrifice your voice to keep the peace. Sometimes the most valuable thing you can offer is the truth that nobody else will tell.
2. **Learn from difficult people, but don't become them.** Working with Glenn was like attending an unconventional business school. He took massive risks, made bold moves, and showed me how high-stakes business operates. But I also witnessed how his wealth and power damaged his relationships. Study the strategies of successful people, even difficult ones, while rejecting the behaviors that

harm others. Your character is the foundation everything else builds upon.

3. **Be gentle with yourself if you're in a difficult relationship.** A difficult boss might drain your energy from nine to five. A toxic partner infiltrates every corner of your existence. Abuse dismantles your reality until you question your own worth. For years, I lived a nightmare while maintaining a successful career. If you're in this situation now, don't feel like something's wrong with you, or that what you're living isn't bad, because you can't leave yet. It took me years. The path out isn't linear. Some days you'll advance, others you'll retreat. But keep listening to that small voice inside that refuses to give up. And when you can, reach out for help.

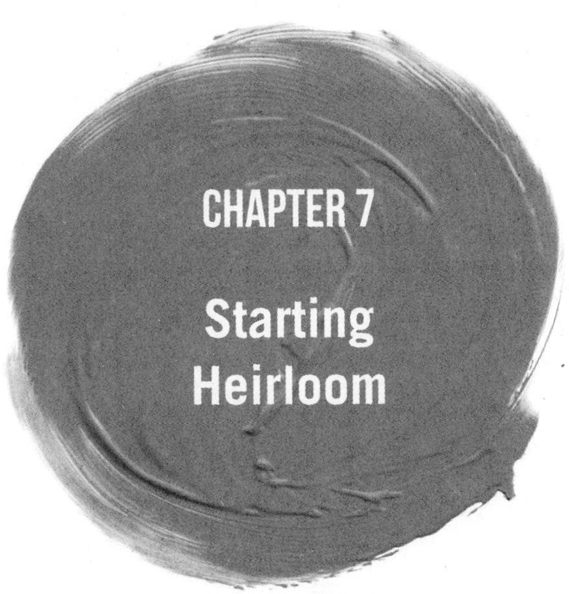

CHAPTER 7

Starting Heirloom

Out of all the cities in the area I could have chosen to move to, the reason I settled on Louisville was because it was home to one of the best high schools in the area. Trinity High School was an all-boys prep school where Brady had to wear a necktie and sports coat every day and study hard. Scholastically speaking, it was excellent. Brady had always skated by just fine with charm and wit, but here, that didn't cut it. He had to apply himself. And he hated it.

"Mom, please. Let's go back to Tennessee," he'd beg. I was paying an arm and a leg for that school, so I wasn't thrilled when he refused to study.

Now, I know what you might be thinking. I realize I have said about a hundred times that I didn't need an education to do what I do. And that's true. I've always believed no one can teach you to have taste. That part—the creative instinct—either you have it or you don't. And I learned everything else the hard way.

But here's what started to hit me as I got older. If I had graduated from high school and gone on to get a college degree in something practical, I'd have had something to fall back on when times got hard on my journey as an entrepreneur. Because the truth is, when you work for yourself, there are no guarantees. I've made money and lost money, sometimes in the same year. That's just part of being an entrepreneur. It's thrilling, yes, but it's not exactly steady. It's hard to build a safety net when your income goes up and down like a yo-yo. And going through things like a divorce, or getting pregnant when you don't expect it, or having to get out of a bad relationship—all of that just drove the point home. Life can change on a dime. And when it does, you'd better have a foundation to stand on. I didn't. I had to hustle my way through it every single time.

With each new venture, I started wondering, *What if this business fails? What if the next one doesn't work? What do I have to fall back on?* It became a real anxiety, especially as I got closer to fifty and realized I didn't have Social Security or a pension coming. There was no backup plan.

That's why I started pushing Brady harder. I wanted him to have something I never had: Security. Options. Stability. I was going to aim the arrow higher for him than I'd aimed for myself. The truth is, I'd never been held accountable to much of anything. My mother let me make all my own decisions, even when I wasn't mature enough to know what I was doing and ditched class to open a clothing store. I was trying to do it differently with my own son, even if he didn't understand it yet.

After a rough start, Brady turned it around and started applying himself in school. I was proud of him; I could see that it was still tough for him to no longer be in Oneida. I wanted to help ease the transition. Now that he was a teenager and starting to be a little independent, I knew he wanted to make a bit of cash. And that's when the idea came to me.

• • •

I'd brought a lot of my big furniture from the old house. Most of it just looked heavy and formal. It didn't fit the new space, especially not the eat-in kitchen. So I thought, you know what? I'm going to paint that old dining table, give it a lighter, more casual look. It was dark wood, really traditional, but I figured if I painted it white, it would feel a little fresher in the new space.

It wasn't just about decorating. This move wasn't just a new zip code: It was me trying to get back to myself, which was a process. Brady wasn't the only one struggling at first; I was too. I was completely alone in Louisville. No friends, no family. I'd cry after he'd go to school, then wipe my face and get on with the day. And painting, something I'd always loved, felt like a step in the right direction. It made me feel like me, and it brought beauty and control back into my life.

So one day, after picking Brady up from school, I stopped in to a little shop and grabbed a can of chalk paint. I took it home and painted the table white. Just experimenting, really. Then I posted a photo of it on Facebook. And that's when the questions started rolling in. People were commenting, "That's beautiful! How did you do that?" Remember: This was back when Facebook was just pictures—no videos or tutorials. A bunch of my friends complimented the picture, and then people I didn't even know started chiming in. I couldn't believe it. Folks in California were seeing this table and asking about it. I didn't understand how—I didn't know the first thing about how social media worked back then. But that one picture got a lot of attention.

I didn't think what I'd done was all that unique. I'd grown up watching my mom paint furniture. It was normal to me. I just figured, *Doesn't everybody paint furniture?* But clearly, they didn't.

Next, I decided to paint another formal dining table. It was a beautiful Henredon, Sheridan style, but it had seen better days. The top was damaged from a candle, and I figured, well, I've got nothing to lose. It was either getting tossed or given away, so I pulled out that same white chalk-style paint and just went for it. Painted the table, painted the chairs, and even painted a buffet I had that didn't match anything. It was a total hodgepodge of pieces, but in that house—which had a gorgeous white-paneled dining room and these beautiful drapes—it all came together beautifully. I took a picture and posted it on

Facebook. Once again, people started asking questions: "How did you do that?" "What kind of paint is that?"

Then one morning in February 2013, I was flipping through a magazine—back when people still had actual magazines lying around—when I came across this ad for Annie Sloan Paint. It wasn't just an ad, really. It was one of those editorial-style things with a picture of her sitting on a sofa, and here I was, sitting on my own sofa, coffee in hand, just staring at it. As I read her story, I thought, *Well, now, wait a minute. She's got a background in furniture and design . . . I've got that. She grew up painting things . . . So did I.* We actually had a lot in common. And I remember thinking, *Too bad I didn't start a paint line. That would've been a good one for me.*

But the more I sat there with it, the more the wheels started turning. At first, I thought chalk paint had already had its moment—like maybe I'd missed the boat. But here I was, posting painted furniture on Facebook and getting flooded with questions: "What paint did you use?" "How'd you do that?" "Can you teach me?" And I thought, *Maybe this thing's not over. Maybe people still want this—and maybe they want to learn how to do it too.*

That was the moment it clicked. *Maybe I should start my own paint brand, and instead of just selling the product, I'd actually teach people how to use it too.* Nobody else was doing that.

That was my brain-spark moment. Brady was home from school in the afternoons and didn't really know what he wanted to do yet, so I thought, *Perfect. He can help me. We'll just play around with it, see where it goes.* I was still traveling back and forth to New York for my work with Glenn, but when I was in Louisville, this would be our little side project.

I remembered that back when I had the floor covering store in Oneida, we used to sell paint. And I was pretty sure we'd bought it from a company in Louisville. The brand was called Gray Seal. That much I remembered.

So I got on the internet, started poking around, trying to track it down. Turns out Gray Seal had belonged to a company called Progress Paint. But Progress Paint had been sold years ago—bought by a company out in California called California Coatings. I dug up a number and called them.

A woman answered. I told her I was looking for a company called Progress Paint. She confirmed that they'd bought them.

"All right, well, thank you so much," I said, ready to hang up.

But before I could, she added, "Wait—there's still a small part of that family business operating in Louisville. You should reach out to them. Their name is Lanning. The business is Lanning Chemical. And what you're asking for is 'toll-made products.'"

Now, this was the pivotal moment. If this woman hadn't answered the way she did, none of what came next would have happened. I probably would have just thought I'd come up with a nice idea I couldn't execute, and cut my losses. I didn't know where to go to make paint, much less how.

But now I had two clues: a company name in the vicinity, and the language to ask for what I needed. I'd never even heard that term before—*toll-made products*.

So I called the Lannings. A young man answered, and I introduced myself. I told him I used to be a Gray Seal retailer in Oneida, Tennessee, and that there was a salesman named Charles who used to call on me and wear taps on his shoes.

"That was my dad's best friend," he answered.

"Are you kidding me?" I shot back.

This guy, whose name was Aaron, told me his dad, Nick Lanning, was the chemist at their plant. "Would you come down and meet us?" he asked.

A few days later, I put on a suit, got in my white car, and headed down to the Lannings' paint plant. In my head, I imagined a big stainless-steel facility, modern, spotless—something like a pharmaceutical lab. I made sure I looked professional.

On the way, I stopped to buy a can of chalk paint to show them what I wanted. I figured if I was going to make paint, I'd want to start with the leader in the market. And back then, everybody was paying $40 a quart for Annie Sloan Paint. I'd never used it, but I assumed it was the best, got it, and drove on to the Lannings', still picturing this high-tech factory.

Oh my, was I wrong.

First off, the place was in the hood. Literally. It was in a part of Louisville that looked like something out of a post-apocalyptic movie. There was black chain-link fence around the perimeter. The building looked boarded up and they had to buzz me in through a gate. I stepped into this little office—maybe 10 by 10 feet—crammed with three desks buried under papers and files stacked 2 feet high. You couldn't even see the surface. I was all dressed up and feeling incredibly out of place.

Aaron walked in and introduced himself, soon followed by his dad, Nick, the chemist. I was standing there in my suit, holding a can of Annie Sloan, thinking, *Well . . . here we go.*

"Do you know what chalk paint is?" I asked Nick.

"Nope, never heard of it," he answered.

And I thought, *Well, here's where this thing falls apart.* I figured the next words out of his mouth would be something like, "We'll need a chemical analysis," and then it'd be, "That'll be $50,000." I was ready to chalk it up as a dead end. At least I could close the loop in my head and move on.

But then—he took the lid off the can, sniffed it, then sniffed it again. He leaned in close, really smelled it, gave it another look, and went, "Oh! I can make that."

Just like that.

"That's just flattened-off house paint," he explained.

I blinked. "How do you know that?"

"Well, when you've done this as long as I have, you know the resin," he said. "I just know what resin they're using."

And I thought, *Well, all right, then.*

We shook hands right there. No contract, no red tape—just a good old-fashioned handshake and a deal. He said, "We'll make you some. We'll take it out to our retail store on Shelbyville Road, and my brother will tint it in whatever colors you want."

Suddenly I had access to the whole rainbow, any color I wanted. These guys were just going to whip up this miracle paint for me like it was no big deal. It almost seemed too good to be true. And that's how we left it.

The whole thing was so unexpected, I didn't even ask how much it would cost or how many gallons I had to commit to. I was still thinking we were in the "talking about it" phase.

I wasn't sure the paint would actually materialize—I wondered if these guys would just forget about it. After all, we'd only shook on it. But I was excited enough about the idea to create a color card with fifty shades of bright, beautiful hues for furniture. I made the card myself using a graphics program on an old CD drive. I wasn't a graphic designer, but it turned out beautiful—a black background with all these vibrant colors I'd named myself. I posted it on Facebook too. At this point, the whole enterprise still felt pretty abstract, but the color card started to make it feel more real. And then I got a message.

A woman with whom I went to high school messaged me on Facebook. "Is that paint?" she asked. "Can I get some of it?"

Now, technically, it wasn't really paint yet. But in my head, it was going to be.

"Yes, it is," I said.

"I'd like to buy some," she told me.

"Do you paint furniture?" I asked.

"I rattle-can stuff," she said.

"Rattle can? You've never actually painted furniture?" I asked.

"No," she said. "But I've got a booth down at the antique mall in our hometown."

"All right, then," I said.

She asked how much it'd cost, and I told her I'd call her back. Truth was, I didn't know yet—I needed time to figure it out. So I got online and went over to Annie Sloan's website. I looked at her wholesale pricing, the sizes she was offering, what it cost to become a retailer—anything I could learn.

It looked like $1,200 was the wholesale buy-in, so that's what I told Charlotte when we spoke again.

I told her, "It's not ready yet, but as soon as it is, I'll bring it down to you. I'll bring Brady to see his dad and drop it off while I'm there."

She agreed. It was February, and I wondered if she was planning on using her tax refund to get this. People in Oneida don't come from money—I know because I'm from there too—and I worried $1,200 might be a stretch for her, but we'd cross that bridge when we got there.

A few weeks later, I finally got the paint. I pulled it all together, made labels from stickers, poking my finger in the paint to dab a dot of color on top of the lid. It was about as old school as you could get.

I packed it all up and drove it down to Charlotte's. On a Sunday afternoon, I sat on the floor of her house on top of a red-and-white checkered plastic picnic cloth. Charlotte sat on the couch, smoking a cigarette, while I painted three tables on the floor and showed her how to use the paint and wax. I left all the products with her, went over the instructions, and just hoped for the best.

She brought me $1,200 in cash. Before I left, I turned back to her and said, "If you can't sell this stuff, I'll buy it back. I don't want you to be stuck with a bunch of paint." I meant it.

About two weeks later, my phone rang.

"I've got a reorder," she said.

"A reorder?" I couldn't believe it.

"Yeah. A $258 reorder," she said. "People love your paint, girl, they love it down here. They're using it on everything. I'm calling it Paula's Paint."

She sent me a photo of her display: It was a chicken wire cabinet—an old jelly cabinet made of rough sawmill lumber, with no glass in the door, just wire. She had all the jars of paint sitting inside it. Above the cabinet hung a two-man crosscut saw on the wall. Real country.

That picture became my first marketing photo. I started posting it online along with a little description of how to become a retailer. I didn't have a website yet, so I used eBay as a stand-in. I listed the paint colors, showed the cans, and wrote in the description: *Want to become a retailer? Send me an email.*

And just like that, Heirloom Traditions Paint was born.

1. **Aim your child's arrow higher than your own.** I know it sounds hypocritical—me, a high school dropout, forcing Brady into a fancy private school with ties and sports coats. But I did it so that he would never feel the fear I did every time life threw me a curveball, whether that was a divorce, an unexpected pregnancy, or a business that tanked. I wanted better for Brady. I wanted him to have options I never did. So when you're making those tough parenting decisions that have your kids rolling their eyes and calling you unfair, remember this: Sometimes love looks like setting a bar they think is too high, because you've seen what happens when there's no bar at all. Your job isn't to make them comfortable today, it's to make them ready for tomorrow.
2. **Your next great business idea could be hiding in plain sight.** Your most valuable skills are sometimes the ones you don't even recognize as special. Pay attention to those moments when people ask, "How did you do that?" with genuine curiosity, or when they say, "I could

never do that," and you think, *Really? But it's so simple!* That disconnect—between what feels basic to you and magical to others—that's your business sweet spot right there. I couldn't believe people were so shocked about painted furniture, because I'd been doing it my whole life, but their reactions are what made me see there was an opportunity there.

3. **The first sale might happen on a picnic cloth.** My first customer wasn't a stranger from a fancy showroom—it was a high school classmate in Oneida with a booth in an antique mall. I sat on her floor on a red-and-white picnic tablecloth, painted three tables, and explained how to use the products including the wax formula I made. That sale didn't look glamorous—but it was everything. That's how you start: one person, one product, one honest conversation at a time. Don't wait for the "perfect" customer or setup. Start where you are, with who you know, and watch it grow from there.

CHAPTER 8

Scaling Up

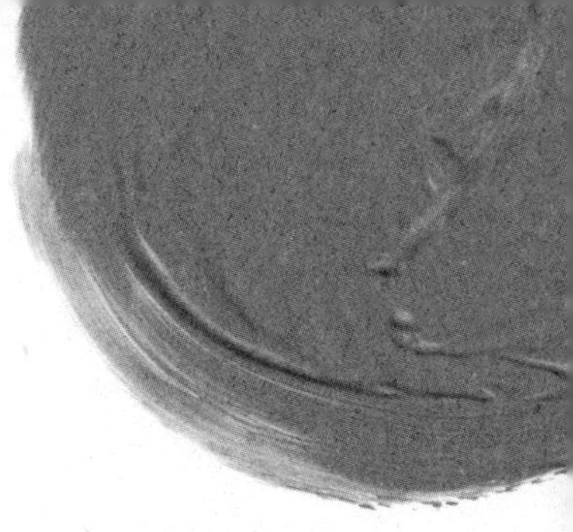

Remember, this was all for Brady. Well, he wasn't thrilled at first.

"Paint? I don't want to be in the paint business!" he protested.

"Well, you don't have to make paint, you just help me package it up," I told him. I honestly wasn't thinking of it as something for me. I was doing it as a sidebar for him. Just for fun money, nothing to do with reality here. Initially, my goal was to sell $100 worth of paint a day. I figured if I could hit that, I'd get $3,000 a month—enough to buy more, give Brady a bit of cash, and keep things moving. That'd be $30,000 or $40,000 a year.

I realized we'd have to scale up when somebody else joined our operation.

• • •

Meeting Craig would change my life in several crucial ways, though I had no way of knowing when we first connected on Match.com.

After Brady and I got settled in Louisville, I figured it was time to try something I hadn't done in a long time: date. It had been a couple of years since I'd freed myself from the toxic hold of my previous relationship. I was ready. And not just to date, but to try to find someone solid. I wanted a man with substance. Someone who'd built something of his own and wouldn't be intimidated that I was trying to do the same. The problem was, I didn't know a soul in Louisville, and I wasn't exactly going to find my soulmate browsing floor wax at Lowe's. I worked all day and didn't go to bars. So I created a dating profile, and that's how I saw Craig's picture.

He looked kind, polished, and put together. I shot him a message, we started talking, and eventually we agreed to meet for a casual lunch at P.F. Chang's.

The conversation was good. I liked him. But when we said goodbye, I figured I'd probably never see him again. He worked out of town a lot, and our schedules were crazy. So I mentally filed it away as a nice afternoon that wasn't going anywhere.

But wouldn't you know, not even an hour later, I started to feel sick. Really sick. This sharp pain hit me in the side like a knife. Next thing I knew, I was in the ER with a ruptured appendix. I was out of it for three days straight. When I finally came to and got home, I checked my phone, and there was a sweet little text from Craig thanking me for the lunch.

It had been days, though, and I figured the window had closed. I didn't answer. *Too bad*, I told myself.

Flash forward a few months, and I'm standing at the register in a restaurant in Lexington when I look up—and there he is. Craig. Walking right past me.

"Hi, how are you?" I asked with a big smile.

"Hi—I'm on a date," he answered hurriedly and kept walking.

Well, here was definitive proof we'd missed our chance. I was disappointed, but I'd been through worse.

When he emailed me not long after asking if I wanted to go out again, I was surprised and cautiously pleased. I said yes. And then didn't hear back from him. Total radio silence.

Well, fine; it looked like the universe was making it real clear we simply weren't meant to be. Especially compared to most of my previous dating experiences, when men seemed to just turn up on my doorstep.

Then I had a dream.

In it, I was praying—really praying—asking God, "Why do I keep choosing the wrong men? Why haven't I met the right one?" And as clear as day, Craig's face popped up in my dream. I laughed out loud when I woke up. I thought, *God, him? The man who didn't even follow up after asking me out?*

I texted him. "I had a dream about you."

He wrote back instantly. "A racy dream?"

"No," I said, "a sweet one."

We went out again, and we've been together ever since.

I really do believe God sent me Craig—or rather, sent me to him—when his face appeared to me in that dream. Craig turned out to be my person. He showed me that after all the hardship of my previous relationship, I could fall in love again, and that that love could be kind and good. He's my husband now. But first, he became my business partner.

Well, not immediately, of course. When we first started dating, Craig was vice president at Delta Dental, running a huge chunk of their group insurance plans. It was solid, real corporate life, and he didn't worry about money. Meanwhile, I was still working for Glenn.

But Craig played a big part in the early days of the paint business. Not long after we got serious, he moved in with me. He had a lot of big furniture. They were beautiful pieces, but they didn't all fit seamlessly into my world. So we ended up buying a house together to make space for our combined lives. Just as my mom had always known how to refurbish or paint over furniture to give it new life, I took a second look at his furniture and saw how I could transform it to fit with mine. One of the first pieces I tackled was the beautiful old Henredon dining table I mentioned before, the second painted piece I shared online.

Craig also had a leather sofa and chair in storage—gorgeous pieces but completely faded. I thought it was such a shame they were hiding out, and I tried everything I could find to bring the fabric back to life: leather conditioners, feeds, oils—stuff from Home Depot, Lowe's, car detailing shops. They'd make the leather look good for a couple hours, but then it would dry back out and turn this awful shade of pumpkin. Nothing worked. I even called a friend who reupholstered car seats, and he said he could recolor them—for $3,000. Well, I wasn't going to do that.

So I channeled my dad and went into scientist mode. I started playing around with different formulas and came up with something that actually soaked in, bonded with the leather, and brought it back to life. When I applied it to the sofa, it looked amazing. I did the chair, then the ottoman. The whole set looked brand new. And that was my first real product—even though I didn't know it yet. At the time, I just stuck the formula in my back pocket and thought, *Maybe one day I'll do something with this.* I snapped a photo of that transformation and put it on Facebook too.

Then Brady and I started actively making and selling paint. I'd rented this little 1,200-square-foot flex space because the mess was too much for the house. Every day, I'd pick Brady up from school, and we'd work in that little space, filling orders, putting labels on cans, loading them in my truck, and hauling them over to the post office.

Craig encouraged us, but he wasn't an active part of the process. Then one Thursday afternoon, while I was making wax, my phone rang. It was Craig. "I've just been let go," he told me.

I was stunned. Craig was fifty-five and thinking he'd retire from this job. I asked if he was serious, and he said, "I don't kid about this." He told me he had thirty days' severance, $100,000 in his 401(k). But that was it. It was a terrifying prospect for someone so close to retirement, who'd likely struggle to get rehired.

The words came out of my mouth before I'd really processed them. I told him I couldn't hire him in this paint business, because it wasn't making enough to pay me, let alone him.

"But there's something here," I told him. "Maybe you could come on board with me. We could try to turn this into something." He laughed.

The next time I saw him, he was sitting on the couch, looking shell-shocked. I sat down with him and gently repeated my offer.

"I know this sounds crazy, but come into this business with me," I said. Between his 401(k) and my savings, we could start something.

He laughed again and laid out his reality. Between alimony to his ex, paying for his daughter's wedding, and setting money aside for his sons' college funds, he had expenses coming out of his ears. "You have no idea what I'm up against," he said.

"No, I don't," I answered, "but let's do this."

It took a few more weeks to convince him, but finally, he relented. He started coming by every day, helping me fill orders, which had grown to $400 or $500 a day by then.

That's when the reality sank in: My little side project with Brady wasn't just a hobby anymore—it had to become our lifeline. With Craig's corporate career suddenly gone at fifty-five, and my inconsistent income from working with Glenn, we were staring down a cliff edge. Between his alimony payments, kids' college funds, and our mortgage—by then we'd moved in together—we needed something stable fast. The paint business that had started as an afternoon activity with my son to make some pocket money was suddenly our best shot at a future.

I never planned on becoming a paint entrepreneur at this stage in my life, but here we were, two middle-aged people betting everything on cans of chalk paint and homemade wax cooked on my stove. I looked at Craig packaging orders in our tiny rented space, and I knew there was no going back. We had to turn these $500 days into something that could actually support us both.

It was sink or swim. It was real.

• • •

Though it was still modest, the business took off faster than I expected. It was becoming harder and harder to keep up with the orders. At first, Brady and I were loading all the paint cans into my truck and driving them to the post office ourselves. But before long, I was filling that truck to the brim and still had more to ship, so the post office had to start picking them up from us. And the messages were rolling in—little mom-and-pop shops on Facebook and eBay wanting to carry our paint. Within fifty days, I'd signed up fifty retailers, each one putting down $1,200 just to get started.

And more and more people were joining our Facebook page too. From day one, I'd always encouraged everyone—retailers and customers alike—to share their before-and-after photos on social media. "Don't forget the before!" I'd always say. The before was just as important as the after. That's what showed the real magic of the transformation. It proved how well the product worked.

It all looked like success on paper. But the reality? We weren't making money. Not even close. For months, we couldn't afford to pay ourselves, and I had to start selling off some land I had just to stay afloat. Part of the problem was that the paint we were selling at the time was a two-step process—paint first, then seal with wax. Simple enough to me, but to the average customer? Confusing. We made a video to explain it and sent it to our retailers, thinking that would do the trick. But either they didn't bother showing it, or no one watched.

Worse, most of these small retailers didn't have the first clue about e-commerce. They might've had Facebook pages, but they posted maybe once a month. They weren't connecting with customers. They weren't telling the story of the product. And without that, the paint just sat on their shelves.

That's when I had two crucial realizations.

The first was that we had to market differently. It was 2014, and the world had already moved online. Gone were the days of magazine ads and mailers. Now it was social media, blogs, email marketing, and video content. Back in Oneida, I'd never had to market that way—people came to me because they knew me. And when I worked for Glenn, he brought in the customers, not me. But now? We were online. That meant learning a whole new game.

So I tried to teach my retailers. I put together big three-day marketing seminars with motivational speakers and the whole nine yards. I was pouring my heart—and my money—into helping them succeed. But no matter what I did, they just didn't get it. Eventually, I threw in the towel.

If the little shops couldn't move my product, maybe the big guys could. I started pitching to major retailers and their networks. I figured they had the muscle and reach to get our paint into more homes.

That brought me to my second big realization. We had to ditch the two-step paint process. None of those big-box employees were going to explain wax and sealers to customers wandering down the paint aisle. If we wanted to scale, we had to simplify.

So I got to work—right over my kitchen stove. I started mixing and testing, playing around with a new idea: a one-step paint. Something that would bond like crazy, have the sealer built right in, and stick to anything—wood, metal, fabric, leather, you name it. No sanding. No priming. No waxing. Just open the jar and go. I took the idea to a chemist, and together, we refined it into what became our flagship: Heirloom Traditions All-In-One Paint.

We finally got it on the shelves at the big retailers and thought we'd made it. But even then, the money wasn't coming in the way we expected. Getting into those stores was expensive. We were shelling out tens of thousands of dollars just to be seen—$40,000 every six months just to attend their trade shows, not to mention the fees just to have our product placed on the shelves. We were working nonstop and still barely keeping the lights on.

And by then Craig wasn't the only one out of a job: I'd stopped working for Glenn to dedicate myself fully to Heirloom.

We had to come up with a new system.

1. **What starts as a side hustle can become your salvation.** I thought I was just doing something lighthearted with Brady—mixing up paint in our little flex space and making a bit of "fun money." My goal was $100 a day, enough to keep him busy and maybe buy a new pair of shoes now and then. But life has a way of upping the stakes when you're not looking. When Craig lost his job, this little paint project became our lifeline. We didn't have time to overthink it. We had to bet on ourselves. Scaling up wasn't some business plan—it was survival. That's how you know you're onto something: when it stops being a hobby and starts carrying real weight.
2. **Necessity doesn't just spark invention—it forces clarity.** The moment we knew we had to make this thing work, I looked around and realized: We were making it too complicated. Nobody wanted a two-step paint process. Not the customers, not the retailers. They weren't going to wax anything. So I did what I always do—I got scrappy. I started experimenting, cooking up what would become our

All-In-One Paint. No primer, no sealer, no sanding. Just open the jar and go. The truth is, I probably wouldn't have pushed that hard if we hadn't been up against a wall. Sometimes your biggest breakthroughs come when your back is against it.

3. **Love doesn't always walk in the front door.** After the kind of relationship I'd come out of, I wasn't sure I'd ever trust someone again. But I knew I was ready to try—and more importantly, I knew what I *wouldn't* settle for. Craig didn't sweep me off my feet. He missed a few cues, and so did I. But when his face appeared in that dream, I knew it meant something. It was peaceful and real. Sometimes love can show up gently, without fireworks, and be everything you'd hoped for.

CHAPTER 9

Ditching the Middleman

By 2018, our sales were decent, but we were about to go broke. Our entire strategy was focused on retail channels—mainly hardware store chains, with some mom-and-pop shops mixed in. We still weren't selling online.

I was fixated on retail for one simple reason: I wanted people to physically see our paint cans and decide which colors spoke to them. Creating professional color cards would have cost upward of $100,000 for just a handful of shades—a price tag we simply couldn't afford. Having our actual product on shelves seemed like the perfect workaround.

That's why I'd worked so hard to get our paint into Hardware Retailers, which I believed would solve everything. This Hardware Retailers is a cooperative that supplies thousands of small, independently owned shops around the country. When you get a product into their system, it becomes available through their warehouse and trucking network—giving small stores access to national distribution they couldn't manage on their own.

My goal was to get our paint into those stores—shops with committed staff, real staying power, and dedicated inventory—unlike the smaller mom-and-pops I'd started out with, which were shutting down faster than new ones were opening. When I went to my first Hardware show, we had a 10-by-10-foot booth tucked into a corner near the women's restroom. I was wedged between giants like Valspar and Benjamin Moore. They had massive setups with plush carpet, coordinated lighting, and polished banners. I had a little wooden display cabinet wrapped with a homemade vinyl sign and a basic point-of-sale system we'd cobbled together. In my mind, it looked like a craft fair table compared to theirs.

Around that same time, I got invited to a small event where the owner of National Recreational Retailers was speaking. After his talk, his buyer drove in to see us in person, and before I knew it, we had our products going into eighty-two of their locations across the country.

Getting into both Hardware Retailers and National Recreational Retailers felt like our big break. We'd invested thousands designing custom end-cap displays—those attention-grabbing setups at the end of retail aisles—so that customers would spot our cans instantly. I proudly announced the news to our Facebook page, which had grown to a couple hundred thousand followers by then. I directed them to the store locations around the country so they could see our products in person. "Pick them up, look at them, hold them, buy them," I wrote.

But people started calling to say they couldn't find them. "I've been to National Recreational Retailers, and they don't have your product," one person wrote.

At first, I couldn't believe it. "It's definitely there," I'd insist. "We designed an end cap for their main floor. It should be sitting right there."

But it wasn't.

What made this particularly maddening was that we had shipped directly to each individual store—not to a central warehouse where items might get lost. Each store had received our shipment. Where had all that paint gone?

I decided to investigate myself. I drove to the store and asked the manager about our paint. His answer was a flat "No, we don't have it." When I explained that we'd shipped an entire end-cap display directly to them, he simply shrugged. "Don't have it."

Standing in that National Recreational Retailers store, staring at the empty space where our products should have been, I felt my stomach drop. But things were about to get even worse.

One day, someone in our Facebook group posted that all our products were on sale for 50 percent off at the National Recreational Retailers website.

I stared at my screen in disbelief. They weren't supposed to sell our products online at all—not even a single can. They were strictly boots-on-the-ground retailers. That was the explicit agreement we had made, the contract I had signed. Our paint was meant to be displayed and sold in physical stores where people could see it, touch it, feel it. That was the whole point.

I immediately called their buyer. "Wait a minute," I said. "You can't do this." I reminded her that I had sold to them at wholesale, plus given them an additional discount off wholesale specifically because they were brick-and-mortar retailers. I had invested $10,000 in those end-cap displays. I'd spent another $20,000 for our products to be featured in their "Sam's All" catalog that went out to campers across the country.

And now I was way underwater financially, with nothing to show for it. The worst part? I later discovered they had never even put the products on their store shelves. Not a single can. They had taken our discounted merchandise and immediately diverted it to their website, undercutting us and every other retailer.

And National Recreational Retailers wasn't the only one pulling these stunts. Around the same time, a woman reached out about seeing our paintbrush on Amazon. I was confused—we didn't sell on Amazon. "No, it's your brush," she insisted. I asked to see it, and she sent a photo. It was actually a Chinese knockoff, not our brush at all.

But while investigating this, I stumbled upon something far more disturbing. I found our actual brushes listed on Amazon—fifteen different listings of them. This made no sense. We had strict agreements with our retailers that they couldn't sell our products online.

I'd never heard of the top seller of our brushes. Who were they? How did they get so much of our inventory? I ordered one of our brushes from them just to track the source.

The package arrived from the exact location of the Hardware Retailers' warehouse. It wasn't a coincidence. I checked our sales figures and discovered that this mysterious "Hardware Retailers" was our number one retailer. Yet in all my years of attending trade shows and meeting with retailers, I'd never once met them.

Then I got it. This was a storefront owned by Hardware Retailers! They were buying our products at wholesale prices, getting additional discounts, charging us warehouse fees, and then selling directly on Amazon—all while hiding behind another storefront.

The entire retail strategy I'd built my business on was crumbling around me. When we got another big order from a different retailer for upward of one hundred locations—on paper, an even bigger opportunity than National Recreational Retailers had been—all I could think was, *They're going to do exactly the same thing to us.*

That's when it hit me. Why didn't I just become the only seller of my own products?

• • •

We were a small but robust team by then. Craig was our CFO, and we had a handful of employees, including our bookkeeper.

I walked into her office and spotted the Tractor Supply order sitting on her desk. "Tear it up," I told her.

"What? We need the money," she answered.

"No, I'm not doing it," I said.

I'd built Heirloom Traditions on this idea that beautiful, transformative paint should be accessible to everyone—not just professional designers or contractors. What was the point if my potential customers, the women who found me on Facebook, couldn't find the product?

"You learn how to do digital ads," I told her. "I'll learn how to make videos. I'm going to turn this camera on and tell the people in our group that today is the last day they ever have to worry about where to get the paint. I'm going to ship it to them at the discount I was giving these other jerks."

I still remember the feeling of determination I felt walking out of her office, pulling out my phone, and turning my camera on. Live on Facebook, I told the group, "We're going to be more honest from now on, and sell the products directly to you." The whole screen just lit up with hearts everywhere. I told them some of what had gone on, how I'd been misled, and how it was all about to change.

Then I walked into Craig's office and told him. He pushed back, as I knew he would. "We can't cut off all these people that are buying our products," he argued. We were already borrowing money against our own revenue through PayPal loans just to stay afloat. The idea of cutting off our primary distribution channels seemed insane.

But I knew that to continue doing what we'd been doing was even crazier.

"You know what? They're actually blocking us from selling," I shot back.

For this next phase of our business, we had to get lean and mean. It was hard. But we weren't just downsizing. It was the rebirth of the business. A complete reimagining of how we would sell our products and who we would sell them to. Out with retailers, in with direct-to-consumer. No more middlemen taking their cut and controlling our destiny.

Neither our bookkeeper nor I had a formal marketing background, but we dove into the world of social media together. We tried everything—Instagram, YouTube, Pinterest, even hired experts for Facebook and Google ads. We figured it out ourselves.

I'd been making Facebook videos for years at that point, just talking to my followers about how to use our products. I'd built this community of passionate DIYers who loved what we were doing. But I'd never really connected that to sales.

I'd never made it easy for them to buy directly from us. The middlemen—the retailers—were always in the way.

Craig and I had a marketing meeting to discuss our new strategy. I figured I had iMovie on my phone—I'd seen it there—and surely running Facebook ads couldn't be that complicated.

Facebook, we realized, was our sweet spot. It had the visuals. It had our demographic. And most important, it had Facebook Live. That was the game changer. I could go live from my phone, walk people through a cabinet transformation in real time, and answer questions as they came in. It was like having a TV show but better—because it was real.

We created a simple three-second video showing a cabinet before and after painting—nothing fancy. Craig reluctantly agreed to a $1,000 ad budget.

Two days later, Melissa reported that the ad had driven $5,000 in sales. We couldn't believe it, so we tried another ad and increased the budget to $2,000. Much to our surprise, it returned $10,000 in revenue, matching the five times return on our investment. Craig walked into our next meeting and was floored to hear we were on track for $100,000 in sales that month, just from the ads.

That was the beginning of everything. In 2016, we'd hit $1.3 million in sales. In 2017, about $1 million. In 2018, when we made this pivot to direct-to-consumer, we jumped to $4 million. The next year, $10 million.

Marketing, to me, is no different from interior design. When I worked with clients, I never just walked into a house and imposed my taste on them. If a woman told me she loved pink, yellow, and blue, I wasn't going to come in with crimson, gold, and navy just because *I* thought it looked better. That might impress someone flipping through a magazine, but the homeowner would feel like a stranger in her own space. And what good is that? Design, like marketing, is about collaboration. You don't push your vision onto someone—you listen, you pay attention, and you create something *with* them, not just *for* them.

This has always been my approach, and yes, it's where I've butted heads with more than a few marketing folks along the way. They'll say things like, "This is what sells," or, "This is how our content needs to look," and consider the matter closed. And I'll ask them, "Says who?" Because more often than not, they're just projecting their own preferences onto our audience. And our audience? She's not twenty-five. She's not living in a New York loft with perfect lighting and a million-dollar renovation budget. She's middle-aged or older, maybe recently retired, maybe an empty-nester. She's got grandkids and a real life and some outdated finishes. And she's tired of being ignored by brands who think inspiration only comes with a filter.

I can't tell you how many times I've said, "I'm not pivoting to TikTok dances to chase teenagers." But here's the twist: Even without trying to go viral, we *have* gone viral. Our

Facebook group has exploded. We've even reached people on TikTok without intending to. No gimmicks, no trends, no gloss. Just real women in real homes transforming their spaces with a brush and a jar of paint. And that has resonated so much that today, we have more engagement than Sherwin-Williams, Behr, Magnolia Home, even Martha Stewart. These are companies that have been online a decade longer than we have—and with much deeper pockets.

And it's not because we're slicker. It's because we're *real.* That authenticity—the choice to show regular homes and messy befores and imperfect afters—that's what people connect with. Major paint brands won't post "ugly" pictures. They don't want to show a kitchen that's a little cluttered, or cabinets that aren't perfectly styled. But that's the world our customers live in. They don't want Pinterest perfect. They want *possible.* They want relatable. They want to believe, "If she did it, maybe I can too."

I still remember one woman, probably in her late seventies, who emailed us photos of kitchen cabinets she'd painted. She told me she'd never attempted anything like it before, but after watching our videos, she felt confident enough to try.

That's what we were really selling—not just paint but confidence. The belief that you could transform your surroundings, that you could make something beautiful with your own two hands.

1. **When the system stops serving you, have the guts to walk away.** For years, I thought getting into big retailers was the holy grail. We poured time and money into end caps, catalogs, and trade shows—only to find out the stores weren't even stocking our products. Worse, they were breaking contracts, selling our paint online, and undercutting us. I realized no one was looking out for our brand but us. That's when I decided: no more middlemen. If you're building a business and the system you're playing in is stacked against you, don't be afraid to walk away. Sometimes your survival depends on breaking the rules you thought were unbreakable.
2. **The people who believe in you are your best business partners.** Our real breakthrough came when we stopped chasing shelf space and started talking directly to the women who used our paint. I turned on my phone, went live on Facebook, and just started being honest. I shared what was happening behind the scenes and promised they'd never have to hunt for our paint again. The

response was overwhelming. That direct relationship—with real people, in real homes—became the heart of our business. Your most valuable marketing tool isn't a glossy ad. It's trust.

3. **You don't need fancy credentials to figure it out. You just need to start.** Melissa was our bookkeeper. I was a designer-turned-entrepreneur. Neither of us had a background in digital marketing. But together, we taught ourselves how to shoot video, run ads, and build community online. Our first $1,000 Facebook ad brought in $5,000 in sales. That's how we grew. We didn't wait until we were experts. We just started. The lesson? Don't let what you don't know stop you. Get scrappy, get curious, and figure it out as you go.

CHAPTER 10

Staying the Course

After our big breakthrough in 2018, everything started moving faster. That first Facebook ad might've felt like a last-ditch effort at the time, but the results changed everything. Sales soared. We were finally connecting directly with the women who actually used our paint, not just the buyers in stores who never called me back. The Heirloom Traditions Paint community we'd started building online exploded almost overnight. It was all hands on deck, making our company bigger and better and simultaneously more intimate.

You would have thought I had my hands full. But my restless brain had other plans in store.

I didn't set out to invent a travel product. It all started back in 2017, when I was on a red-eye flight to New York, desperate to get some sleep. You know those big fluffy neck pillows everyone uses? Totally useless for me. They always pushed my head forward in the most uncomfortable way. I sat there, exhausted, watching other people's heads roll around like bobbleheads.

I thought to myself, *Man, if I had a string, I could just tie my head back to this headrest.* That's when it hit me. I had a scarf around my neck, so I placed it across my forehead and tied it around the headrest. It was incredible. My head stopped bobbing. I actually slept. Real, restful sleep. On a plane.

When I got home, I couldn't stop thinking about that scarf trick. I pulled out my sewing machine and started tinkering. Eventually, I came up with a slim little pillow with straps that you could tie to the headrest—same concept but way more comfortable. I thought it was clever, so I took it to a local patent attorney to see if anything like it already existed.

Months later, I was frying bacon on a Sunday afternoon when my attorney called. "Paula, I've got your research back on your travel pillow," he said. "Do you know how many travel pillows there are that have been designed in the patent files?"

"Well, I would assume it's extensive," I replied.

"Yours is the only one that works," he told me. "Of all the travel pillows, I think you will get a design and a utility patent on this product."

If you've ever filed a patent, you know that's no small thing. Utility patents aren't handed out like candy. It meant the pillow wasn't just a cute idea—it was truly original.

I couldn't believe it. I didn't have a high school diploma, but I had a US patent. That gave me the confidence to launch the product on Kickstarter. I figured we'd make a little noise and move a few units.

We did $485,000 in forty-five days.

Next thing I knew, I was being asked to go on TV. I ended up on both *The Dr. Oz Show* and *Harry*, Harry Connick Jr.'s talk show. The pillow was also featured on BuzzFeed, and in *The Times* in London. Then came the kicker: a call from the producers at *Shark Tank* asking if I wanted to be on the show. Me—with my little scarf-turned-pillow—on *Shark Tank*. It was surreal.

I was flying all over the place, showing the product at trade shows and pitching it to buyers. I even started talks with WH Smith, the British retailer with stores in airports around the world. They loved it. The plan was to roll it out in twenty-four of their stores, which would've been a dream come true. But it came with a hefty price tag—$1,000 per store, per month, just to be on the shelf. Still, I believed in the product.

I was getting ready to sign the deal when COVID-19 hit. Travel ground to a halt. Luckily, I hadn't mailed that first check yet. It would've been a financial disaster.

Still, I had eighty thousand pillows already manufactured and sitting in storage. I'd put up $280,000 of my own money to make them. Let me tell you, that's a lot of pillows. I decided to sell them myself, online and directly to retailers. The product was simple to ship, and we already had a warehouse through Heirloom Traditions. I thought, why not?

But I hadn't fully thought through just how different that business would be from paint. Different customer base.

Different marketing. Different everything. I couldn't just plug it into our existing paint systems and expect it to go. It started pulling time, attention, and resources away from the business that was actually keeping the lights on.

In my excitement over the pillow's meteoric rise, I almost threw away what was becoming my family's lifeblood. My paint business.

I've always been an ideas person—creative and quick to act. Most of the decisions I've made in business have come from instinct. I get a gut feeling about something—a product, a concept, a direction—and when it feels right, I don't wait around. I move. Fast. I don't spend a lot of time second-guessing or over-planning; I trust that I can handle the hiccups as they come. And to be honest, that approach has worked for me more often than not.

I've had a strong eye for style ever since I was a teenager, and I knew it. That's why I opened my first clothing store at sixteen years old. Later, when I was just starting out designing leather belts and John Schneider asked if I could make him a full leather outfit, I said yes on the spot and figured I'd learn how to make one, even though I'd never made anything beyond accessories. And when I got that million-dollar order for my Sassy line, I didn't have the infrastructure to pull it off, but I said yes anyway and hustled like crazy to find a way to make it happen. That's just who I am. If the spark hits and it feels right, I trust it and jump.

But I'll also be the first to admit that it's not always the safest route. That's why I need a counterbalance—someone who reins me in when I get too swept up in my own momentum.

Today, that someone is my husband, Craig.

Craig is the president and CEO of Heirloom Traditions, and he's the one who handles the money and makes sure we stay in the black—and out of trouble. Where I tend to leap first and look later, Craig is the guy who checks the rules, reads the fine print, and asks the right questions. He's calm, grounded, and meticulous. Nothing gets a green light from him unless it's fully aboveboard.

I'll admit, I'm a little more relaxed when it comes to red tape. If there's a permit that seems like a hassle, I might be tempted to skip it and deal with the fallout later. But Craig always insists, "Let's do it right the first time." And he's absolutely right.

His steady hand keeps our business on course, and his integrity sets the tone for everything we do. You can't overstate how important that is.

Before Craig, for nearly thirty years, that person was my sister, Sherry. She was the steady hand behind the curtain. She handled the books, the taxes, the inventory, the tagging, the day-to-day logistics—every bit of it. We were complete opposites, and that's probably why we worked so well together. I was the extrovert. I was the one out front, chatting with customers, working the floor, dreaming up new product lines. Sherry stayed behind the scenes, taking care of the parts of the business that frankly never interested me. And I never pretended they did. I didn't want to know how to do taxes. I didn't want to learn to track inventory. I wanted to sell, create, and keep the energy flowing.

When we went our separate ways in 2008, everything started to wobble. All of a sudden, I realized I didn't even have a proper inventory sheet. I was so used to her managing that side of things, I hadn't really kept track of what was going on behind the scenes. And that caught up with me.

Now, I don't think you need to be able to do every single job in your business—not at all. What I do believe is that you've got to be honest with yourself about what you're great at and what just isn't your gift. Then you build a team around you—people who actually enjoy doing the things you'd rather not touch—so you can stay in your zone of genius. That's how Sherry and I did it for years. And that's what Craig did for me with Heirloom.

Craig is one of the very few people who can talk me down from an idea once I've got my heart set on it. And that's saying something. I may not always love hearing it in the moment, but over the years I've learned to really listen to him—because when Craig sees a problem, there usually is one. If he can lay it out clearly enough that even I start to see the cracks, I'll let it go. No drama, no resentment. I just move on.

One of the best examples of that came early on in the Heirloom days, back when we were still getting our feet under us. I had this big idea that we should launch a hemp oil hair-care line. I mean, I was *convinced.* Hemp oil is incredible for moisture and shine, and I'd read that it might even help with hair growth. I got so fired up about it that I went and bought these huge drums of hemp oil and started whipping up shampoo formulas in my kitchen. I gave samples out to friends and customers, and sure enough, people loved it. That just made me more sure I was onto something big.

So I told Craig I was ready to roll it out. Brand it, bottle it, get it on the market.

Well, he just looked at me and said, "Why are we selling shampoo? We make paint."

I tried to argue my way around it, like I usually do. But he kept bringing it back to the same point: We had a paint business to build, and if we wanted it to succeed, we needed to give it our full focus. "You've only got so many hours in a day," he said, "and every minute you spend chasing shampoo is a minute you're not growing Heirloom."

And he was right. As much as I loved the idea, it wasn't the right time—or the right lane. So I dropped it. That's the kind of clarity Craig brings. He keeps me grounded when my imagination tries to run wild.

It was the same story with the travel pillow.

I realized I was chasing the next shiny object, thinking it could be my ticket to something bigger. But Heirloom was already big. It was already working. I just needed to stay the course.

Eventually, I had to face the music. The pillow was a good idea—and I still think it's one of the best products I've ever made—but it just didn't belong inside the paint business. It needed a whole separate team and structure to thrive, and we weren't in a place to give it that. So I made the hard call and donated the remaining inventory to Goodwill.

It was bittersweet, but it taught me a lot. Not every good idea needs to become a business. Not every opportunity is worth chasing if it pulls you too far off track. I've always believed in moving fast, fixing as I go—but in this case, I moved a little too fast and went a little too big.

I'm a product inventor, that's true. But color is my gift.

• • •

When I brought my focus back to Heirloom, everything got sharper.

After our direct-to-customer breakthrough in 2018, we started scaling up. We needed more space. Craig found a 10,000-square-foot building in Taylorsville, about thirty minutes from where we lived. When he first mentioned it, I wrinkled my nose. "Taylorsville? That's a haul." But I agreed to go look.

It turned out to be this big, plain metal building once used as a Navy SEAL dog training center, of all things. Nothing glamorous. Just a giant open space with decent bones. But what it had was five acres. Even if that wasn't enough space long-term, we could add on. We'd have room to grow. We closed on it in November 2019 and started remodeling that month.

And then, just as we were gearing up to move in—boom. COVID-19.

We moved into that building right as the world started shutting down. And you'd think hiring during a time like that would've been a disaster. But something totally unexpected happened.

People lined up outside our door. Actually lined up. Thirty deep, standing outside, résumés in hand, waiting to apply.

It was a total one-eighty from what we'd dealt with in Louisville. Back in the city, we were hiring folks fresh out of heroin rehab programs—because honestly, that's who showed up. Most didn't stay long. They'd come in for a while, then fall off the wagon. It was both heartbreaking and exhausting, like a revolving door that we couldn't stop.

Taylorsville is one of those little bedroom communities that feeds into the city. People live out there because it's peaceful, but almost all the jobs are in Louisville. That means hours every week stuck on Taylorsville Road, watching your life tick by through a windshield.

In Taylorsville, we tapped into a completely different workforce. Moms who wanted to be closer to home. Folks sick to death of traffic. We were offering more than a job—we were offering time back with their families. They came ready to work, skilled and steady.

We poured our energy back into what we knew was working. No more distractions. No more second-guessing. We rolled out new products, better tools, built up the brand stronger than ever. The numbers followed: $10 million, then $30 million a year.

We were focused. We stopped chasing shiny objects and put our hearts right where they belonged.

1. **Not every good idea deserves to be a business.** I've had a lot of ideas over the years—some brilliant, some less so. That travel pillow? It was one of the best things I ever invented. It worked. It had a patent. It made nearly half a million dollars in a matter of weeks. But just because something has legs doesn't mean you should walk away from what's already carrying you. Heirloom was thriving, and I nearly lost sight of that chasing the next shiny object. If you're building something meaningful, don't get distracted by everything that glitters. A great side idea can still wreck a main business if you're not careful.
2. **Speed is your superpower—until it's not.** I've built my entire career on moving fast. Trusting my gut. Saying yes before I had all the answers. And for the most part, that instinct has served me well. But sometimes speed without focus just turns into chaos. What I've learned is this: If you're always in go-mode, you need someone on your team who knows when to pump the brakes. For me, that's been Craig. He's the one who asks, "Is this where

we want to spend our time? Our money? Our energy?" You can be fast and still be thoughtful. Don't confuse motion with momentum.

3. **Stay the course—especially when it's working.** It's easy to chase what's new, especially when you're a creative person. But building something great means sticking with it even when the next big thing is calling your name. Heirloom wasn't just "doing well"—it was changing lives, including mine. I had to remind myself: *This is what matters*. This is what we're building. When I put my energy back into paint, everything sharpened. Our team grew stronger. Our customers showed up louder. And the business took off like never before. If you've got something that's working, nurture it. Give it your whole heart. That's how you turn momentum into legacy.

CHAPTER 11

Full Circle

When I first decided to start making paint in 2014, I had no idea where to begin. Then I remembered we used to sell a brand called Gray Seal back at the old floor covering store Sherry and I ran in Oneida, and after a little digging online, I traced it to a company in Louisville called Lanning Chemical.

I told you: I showed up in a suit, expecting some shiny corporate lab, and instead found a boarded-up building surrounded by a chain-link fence, with stacks of papers 2 feet high piled on desks inside. A real mess. But Nick Lanning, the chemist, took one sniff of the can of chalk paint I'd brought with me and said, "I can make that." And he did.

Nick Lanning is the person who first got my harebrained scheme in motion. Without him, who knows if I would have ever even started Heirloom? At that point it was just an idea for a hobby. If Nick Lanning hadn't taken me seriously that day, I might've shelved the whole idea before it ever became real.

Over the years, as our business grew, I stayed with the people who'd helped me get started. The Lannings had been making our paint since day one. They did a good job for a long time.

But as time went on, their quality started slipping. Whites started coming out stained. Our signature color, Cashmere, would be a shade or two off, and customers started returning products, saying it didn't match. I found out that Lanning Chemical was switching out resins depending on which deals they could get, and I started hearing complaints about sludge in the paint. It wasn't just the product—everything felt off. They couldn't keep track of their books either. One day they'd say we owed them this, the next day it was something completely different. Their office told the story—piles of paper, chaos in every corner.

Nick was getting old and had left the day-to-day operations in the hands of other people, who, it seems to me, had their mind on other things.

Then sometime in 2016, I got the opportunity to put our product into the Hardware Retailers warehouse. I told the Lannings, "Look, I'm taking this line into wholesale. I don't have the margin, since I'm not the manufacturer, to just give a chunk away. But if you give a little and I give a little, we can grow this business faster than what I'm doing selling to mom-and-pop shops."

They said they were on board.

I went to the show, set up our little 10-by-10-foot booth on a corner. Everyone else had these giant banners, big glossy setups, carpeting on the floor. I had a folding table and a roll of burlap wrapped around some particleboard to make it look like something. But we held our own.

At the end of the show, the buyers came over. "We want to place a fifty-thousand-dollar order for the warehouse," one of them said.

I couldn't wait to tell the Lannings. We'd done it. We're going into the warehouse. This product was going to ride out on trucks to major retailers all across the country.

Then Monday morning came.

The office manager at Lanning Chemical handed me a sheet of paper. "Here's the new pricing from the Lannings," she said.

They'd raised our price by 30 percent.

They weren't giving me a nickel—in fact, they were going in the opposite direction. I was floored. I barely had a 30 percent margin to begin with, and now they'd eaten it all. With the wholesale markup I needed to give Hardware Retailers, I was underwater.

"What are you doing?" I asked when I called. "I thought we agreed to meet in the middle."

"Well, you know, raw materials are going up—calcium carbonate, resins, everything," they told me.

I let them talk, but I knew better. Yes, prices were moving, but not like that. I knew the business. I was paying attention.

They were wrong.

So I sat there in a kind of stupor, thinking, *What now?*

Louisville used to be a hub for the paint industry. Most of those companies were gone by then, but I remembered the Lannings had mentioned a few still hanging on. So I picked up the phone and called one called Kelley Technical Coatings. I knew they made pool paint, but I figured it was worth a shot.

I got the CEO, a guy named Bill Lamar, on the phone.

"I know you're good friends with the Lannings," I told him.

"We are," he said. "But business is business. Let's talk."

So I set up a meeting. I drove down with a can of the paint the Lannings made and said, "I need this product. I need it soon. I've got a growing brand, and I need a partner who can keep up." The problem, I explained, was that I didn't have a formula. I asked him if he could reverse engineer it. He said he could. We shook on it. Two weeks later, Kelley Technical Coatings handed me a sample and a price.

It was good. I thought I'd found a solution.

But about three months into the deal, the owner, John Kelley Jr., passed away. He didn't have any children or succession plan. His widow announced she was going to take over the company.

Now I was in a bind. My entire business depended on this new supplier, and I had no idea what its new CEO, John's widow, Elizabeth, would be like.

That scared me. She had every right to walk out that door, close the business, and just like that, I'd lose everything. My whole operation was now tied to her. I didn't have a contract. No guarantees. I'd just shook hands with a man who was no longer living. And now his widow—who hadn't been involved in the business before—was in charge.

What if she decided to raise the prices? What if she decided she didn't want to deal with me at all? I had no idea what would happen, and I didn't like feeling that vulnerable.

Meanwhile, the Lannings were furious with me. They didn't like that I'd left, and I could hardly blame them.

I met Elizabeth soon after. She walked into our meeting in a beautiful suit. We were definitely not cut from the same cloth.

We stayed in business together, and Kelley Technical Coatings continued making us a good product. For a few years, everything went well. Then history repeated itself. Every time I introduced a new paint color, Kelley raised the cost again. Slowly but surely, the price kept creeping up.

I thought, *Man, we've got to be the ones driving this car. We cannot sit in the back seat and just let somebody else steer.* "If we don't figure out how to make paint ourselves, we're going to be at the mercy of other people forever," I told Craig.

"We're too old to start a paint factory, Paula," Craig, always the realist, answered.

But I knew this time, the situation was different. This wasn't starting a hemp shampoo line or getting into travel pillows. This was finding a solution to our lifeblood. So I insisted. "We're exactly the right age to start one. We're old enough to know better. We've got to do this."

So I started researching how to start a paint plant. The problem was, I couldn't find paint people, or at least not the kind who still make paint today. There weren't many who were willing to come all the way out to Taylorsville. It was hard to get a grip on it. I even hired a consultant, tried every angle I could think of.

Then came another obstacle.

There had been a massive freeze in Texas, and the roof of the Dow Chemical plant collapsed. That triggered what they called force majeure, which basically meant nobody new was getting a resin allocation.

And that put a huge bump in the road for me. You can't make paint without resin. No resin, no manufacturing.

So I backed off for a bit. Took a breath. I started to wonder if maybe Craig was right—maybe we were too old to be doing this.

But then I remembered—Elizabeth, Kelley Technical Coatings' new owner—was older than me.

I emailed her and asked to meet. She agreed.

I told her to come down to my office. She showed up with her new CEO in tow, and I sat them both down. I said, "Look, we've always tried to be a great partner. We've never been in any kind of contract. We've just bought what we needed without signing anything. But if it helps, I'll sign a contract. I'll show you what we bought last year, and what we plan to buy next year. That way you don't feel like this is a bump in the road."

And then I told them what I'd actually been building up to tell them.

"I want to pay you. I want to pay you for your expertise. I want to pay for your help to start our own paint operation."

Up until that moment, we hadn't known what they thought of us. We didn't know where we ranked with them. We didn't know if we were a good customer or just a pain in their ass. I mean, their main business was pool paint—not furniture paint like ours. So we always kind of felt like maybe we were just an aggravation. A distraction.

So when I sat them down and told them we were planning to make our own paint—with or without their help—I didn't know how they'd take it.

Well, I found out real quick.

They went white. Just white-faced. Elizabeth didn't say another word. They were not happy. Not at all.

Before they left, we asked if they'd be willing to put something in writing—a contract that laid out what I'd offered in the meeting: what we bought last year, what we planned to buy next year, and some kind of formal agreement so we could move forward professionally.

We never heard a word.

No follow-up. No thank-you email. No "we'll think it over." Nothing. Just silence.

And that's when I knew—we'd hit a nerve.

"They're going to cut us off—we won't even have a supplier," Craig worried.

"Well, we've got to do it anyway," I answered. "We've got to pull the trigger."

Because the truth was, they were making money on us. That's why they went white-faced in the meeting. That's why they said nothing. They knew they might lose us, and they didn't like it.

So from that point on, I walked on eggshells. We tiptoed around them for a while. I gave it time.

A full year passed. Our business was growing fast. We were doing so well, in fact, I won the Woman Entrepreneur of the Year award in 2021, when our brand was ranked the twenty-third largest international production company led by a woman.

One day in mid-2022, I was just sitting at my desk when I decided to get in touch with Elizabeth again. I wanted to up the ante. I was going to ask her to sell me her business.

She was in her mid-seventies by then. I couldn't stop thinking that at her age, it was likely she'd sell the business, and where would that leave me?

I had no idea how many employees she had, or what the company was really worth. I was just guessing—thinking maybe $10 million could buy it. Total shot in the dark.

I sent her an email and asked her if she'd like to go to lunch. I didn't tell her why I wanted to meet. I figured she'd connect the dots. It was a continuation of the conversation we'd started back in my office a year earlier.

We went to lunch, and right away, she came at me with a string of backhanded compliments.

"I saw you won that Woman Entrepreneur of the Year award in Montreal," she said. "What a great award." Their company had sent me champagne and a whole package of congratulations when it happened. "But I don't really like being compared to just women-owned businesses," she continued. "I prefer to be in the mix with men and women, not just women."

I just sat there thinking, *I didn't even know we were competing.*

She kept going, talking about her degrees and credentials, and I realized this conversation was heading somewhere I hadn't expected.

Still, I stayed with it and finally got to the point.

"I just want to continue the conversation we started in Taylorsville. I want to make paint there. But before I move further in that direction, I want to say this to you: I don't want to hurt your business by taking our volume away without giving you the opportunity to plan. I don't want to hurt your people. So if your goal is to sell at some point, I'd like to be the buyer. I'd like to keep your people on."

She looked straight at me. "You're not the buyer," she said.

I sat there, trying not to choke on my food. Then I said, "I think maybe you're assuming I'd just take your business and dump everything on the internet."

"Well, our products don't sell online. They sell through trade shows and traditional distribution channels," she answered.

"We can do that. Before you ever heard of me, I was already selling to hardware chains. I've done the trade shows. I know the full kit and caboodle," I explained.

And she said, "Oh, I didn't know that."

We talked for fifteen minutes, shook hands, and I said, "If you want to ever sell your business, I'll connect you with Craig, and you and he can go from there."

She took about two weeks to respond to Craig.

Eighteen months later we were the owners of Kelley Technical Coatings.

We now had eight buildings scattered across a property split by a railroad track, two camps of workers who mostly sat around smoking, waiting for someone else to make the first move. They were used to seasonal work—half a year on, half a year off, still getting paid either way. That wasn't how I did business. I whipped it into shape.

I started cleaning house—remodeling offices, building conference rooms, upgrading every square inch. New equipment. Once I cleared the decks, everything clicked. Orders started pouring in. I moved the products from old-school distributors directly onto Amazon—even though people said you couldn't do it. They said those paints couldn't sell online. I proved you could.

The change was immediate. That gallon of paint they were selling for $51.50 through dealers—they couldn't move it. I put it online and sold it for $149, paid up front, no middleman. That shift alone turned it into a cash cow overnight.

So I made a decision: Sell off the plants and build a whole new setup. We had fifteen acres in Taylorsville. We broke ground on a 30,000-square-foot warehouse with 24-foot sidewalls for shipping and fulfillment—and next to it, a brand-new paint plant with automated mixers and labeling. We needed that scale.

We listed the old buildings. The first plant by the tracks went, then the old dirty one with all the equipment.

You'll never guess who one of the buyers was. It was Nick Lanning of Lanning Chemical, the company I'd left for Kelley Technical Coatings but which had first gotten me started.

The day they came to sign the papers, Nick—who'd been the brain behind it all—was probably eighty-five. Most of the men he'd come up in the paint industry with were gone. After he'd walked in, my chemist came over to him and said, "You're paint royalty in this town."

Then one of the guys from our lab stepped forward and told Nick he had something to show him. He disappeared and returned carrying a pile of old photographs that had been kept in the building for years before we bought it. They were of the men in the paint industry through the years, decades of golf outings, conferences, shop floors. Paint royalty like Nick.

Nick sat at that table, slowly going through the pictures, naming each face. One worked in resin development, another created the formulas we still used. Prewar chemistry. My lab guy pointed at each one and told Nick, "These are the men who built the paint you're still selling today."

When they were ready to leave, I handed Nick the photos. "Take them with you," I said.

I'll never forget the sight of him walking out, holding those photos like treasure. He was carrying the legacy of a generation. And he was walking away with a plant his family could never have built on their own. It filled me with a deep sense of happiness and gratitude that after all these years, I was in a position to help him, the way he had once helped me.

I'll never forget it.

1. **Own your process—or someone else will own your fate.** In the early days, I didn't have the know-how or resources to make my own paint. So I partnered with people who did. But over time, I realized that as long as someone else controlled the product, they controlled the future of my business too. It's OK to start that way. In fact, you may need to. But if you want to grow beyond survival mode, you've got to get behind the wheel. Don't let someone else dictate your margins, your pace, or your standards. Owning your process gives you the freedom to innovate, pivot, and build something that truly lasts.
2. **Don't let fear of rejection stop you from asking for what you want.** When I told Elizabeth I wanted to start my own plant—and later, that I wanted to buy her business—I had no idea how she'd react. But I knew this: Staying silent would only keep me stuck. That conversation was uncomfortable, even painful. But it opened the door that ultimately led to me owning the company. If there's something you want—an opportunity, a partnership, a

shot at something bigger—you've got to ask. You don't have to be aggressive. You just have to be brave. And when someone tells you no? That's not the end of the story. It could be a sign to find another way.

3. **Loyalty doesn't mean staying stuck—it means remembering who helped you rise.** When I walked away from Lanning Chemical, it wasn't easy. But business is business, and I had to leave when quality and trust started slipping. Still, I never forgot who gave me my start. Years later, when I had the chance, I helped Nick and his family buy a piece of the very business they helped me begin. That's what loyalty looks like—it's not about clinging to people out of guilt or nostalgia. It's about circling back when you're able, and lifting others the way they once lifted you.

CONCLUSION

I never dreamed that paint—making it, selling it, or anything to do with it—was what I'd ultimately be doing with my life. And I certainly thought by the time I turned fifty that I'd already achieved most of the big, great things I was meant to do. But starting this business proved otherwise.

If you'd told me years ago that I'd one day be running a multimillion-dollar paint company, I probably would've laughed out loud. Not because I didn't think I was capable, but because it just wasn't on my radar. My life, up to that point, had been full of twists and turns—flooring, furniture, interiors, retail stores, inventions, even a hair-care idea that never saw the light of day. I'd started things, lost things, rebuilt things, and always kept going. But I didn't think *this*—jars of paint—would be the thing that stuck.

And yet here we are. Over $33 million in annual sales. A woman at the helm of one of the only female-owned businesses in the paint and coatings world. They've called me the Queen of Paint, handed me shiny awards, and written headlines about the growth of Heirloom Traditions. And while I'm proud of all that, those aren't the things I think about at the end of the day.

What I think about is that moment when I was new to Louisville, completely on my own, trying to start over and not sure how. I'd already been through so many transformations by then, but this one was the hardest. I had left my hometown—the only place I'd ever really known—because I had to. I was leaving a toxic relationship. I was protecting my son from small-town judgment, from the sideways glances and whispered comments that came with being born to a single mom. This wasn't just a move—it was a clean break. And like every other turning point in my life, it didn't begin with some big master plan.

I didn't realize that mixing paint in my kitchen to give my son something to do and connect with him during a complicated life transition would be the defining transformation of my life.

What I've come to understand is that creativity and reinvention aren't separate things. They're often the same thing in disguise. Every time I tried something new—whether it worked or flopped—I was carving out a path. I was learning. I was shaping a life.

And maybe that's what success really is. Not a dollar figure or a headline, but the ability to look back and say: I stayed curious. I stayed open. I kept creating.

When people ask me how I did it—how I built a business from scratch, how I kept going after making mistakes, how I managed to grow something meaningful—I tell them I didn't have a road map. I just opened a hundred jars. That's what I did, over and over again. I didn't always know what color I'd paint with or what design I'd make. I just knew I had to start.

And ultimately, what I was able to build was always so much bigger than me. Once I put Heirloom Traditions Paint out in the world, I realized we'd created something unique. The energy was different. It was like a feeding frenzy. I had spent years working to get people to walk into physical storefronts. Suddenly, they were banging on my virtual door. People came knocking, and not just with their dollars but with their stories. With their hopes. With their need to feel like they could change something, even if it was just the cabinets in their kitchen.

I saw that people wanted guidance, a voice telling them, "Yes, you can do this." Many of them were going through difficult things—economic hardship, depression, loneliness. And these jars we were offering became something much bigger.

Our customers aren't design experts or social media stars. They're retirees rediscovering joy, moms painting in the garage after the kids go to bed, burned-out professionals longing to reconnect with something real. They're people who thought they needed to tear it all down to start over, only to realize that sometimes all you need is a new coat of paint.

Heirloom Traditions Paint is so much more than a company. It's a movement, and that's thanks to you.

So if there's one thing I hope you take away from my story, it's this: You are never too far gone to become someone new. No matter what chapter you're in, no matter how many wrong turns you've taken, you are never stuck. Reinvention isn't reserved for the lucky or the rich or the young. It belongs to anyone brave enough to pick up the brush.

I've lived a lot of lives. A restless teen with a flair for fashion, a furniture store owner, a burned-out consultant, a single mom, a warehouse hustler, a late-night inventor. And through it all, I kept circling back to one question: "What can I make out of this?"

That's what creativity really is. Not some fancy talent bestowed on the chosen few, or a college degree. It's a decision. A grit. A willingness to see more than what's in front of you. Whether it's an ugly dresser or a broken season of life, it's the stubborn belief that with a little vision and a lot of heart, you can make something better.

Heirloom Traditions Paint was never just about paint. It was about what the paint allowed people to do. It was about seeing women stand taller after finishing their kitchen cabinets. Hearing them say, "I did this myself," with awe and pride. Watching them go from hesitant to unstoppable.

In every can we shipped, I saw a thread that connected us: the homemaker and the businesswoman, the grandmother and the girl just starting out. We'd all been told no. We'd all had to prove ourselves. And now we were reclaiming our space, one brushstroke at a time.

People sometimes ask me what my biggest success has been. They expect a number. A sales milestone. A viral video. And sure, those things matter. But to me, the real answer is simpler: I didn't quit.

I kept going when the odds didn't favor me. When the market changed. When relationships broke. When the money dried up. I kept building, kept believing, kept painting forward. And in doing so, I found something better than success. I found purpose.

If you're holding this book because you're wondering what's next for you, let me tell you this: It doesn't matter where you start. It doesn't matter if you've failed before. All that matters is that you begin. Open the jar. Dip the brush. Take the first step, even if it's messy.

You don't need permission. You don't need perfection. You just need to begin.

So here's to your next chapter. May it be messy and bold and full of color.

ACKNOWLEDGMENTS

To my husband, Craig, thank you for being the calm in the storm and the steady hand at my back. Your love and support have never wavered, even when the path forward wasn't clear. You've stood by me with quiet strength, and I'm endlessly grateful.

To my son, Braden, this journey began because of you. Our move to Kentucky, the business that was born in our kitchen, and the life that's unfolded since were all rooted in love for you. Watching you grow and thrive has been the greatest reward of my life.

To my sister, Sherry, thank you for being my rock and my reality check. Your encouragement, your wisdom, and your loyalty have been a constant light through every chapter.

ACKNOWLEDGMENTS

To my parents, thank you for your love, your presence, and your belief in me, even when I didn't fully believe in myself. Your example helped shape the mother, the woman, and the leader I've become.

To my grandparents, Roscoe and Ruby Kidd, you are the foundation of everything I am. "No" was never part of your vocabulary. You gave generously of your time, your money to support my crazy ambitions, and most importantly, your example. You taught me how to work hard, manage money wisely, prioritize family, and live a life rooted in Christian values. Your legacy lives in everything I do.

To my team, thank you for bringing heart, hustle, and integrity into our mission every single day. I could never have done this alone.

To our incredible customers, thank you for believing in our products, for sharing your stories, and for letting us into your homes and your lives.

And to you, the reader, thank you for opening this book, and maybe even opening your own jar.

ABOUT THE AUTHOR

Paula Blankenship is the founder and CEO of Heirloom Traditions Paint and Camcoat, two nationally recognized brands that have revolutionized the way people transform their homes. A Tennessee native, Paula moved to Kentucky thirteen years ago, knowing no one, with one goal in mind: to give her teenage son Braden a better future through enrollment at Trinity High School. The transition was hard, especially on him. In an effort to ease the pain, Paula began painting in her kitchen. What started as a way to cope quickly turned into a calling.

From those early kitchen experiments came All-In-One Paint, a simplified, all-surface solution that empowered millions of homeowners and DIYers. Through grit, vision, and an unstoppable belief in what could be, Paula built her business into a multimillion-dollar direct-to-consumer brand reaching millions every month. But more than a story of business success, Paula's journey is one of healing, reinvention, and the quiet strength it takes to begin again.

Just Open the Jar is her first autobiographical work, an intimate, unfiltered look at the real life behind the scenes. Part memoir, part manifesto, it's a love letter to transformation, to motherhood, and to trusting that even the hardest chapters can lead to the best parts of the story.